Children's Toys
You Can Build Yourself

Children's Toys You Can Build Yourself

Franklynn Peterson

Prentice-Hall, Inc., Englewood Cliffs, New Jersey

Children's Toys You Can Build Yourself
by Franklynn Peterson
Copyright © 1978 by Franklynn Peterson

Printed in the United States of America
Prentice-Hall International, Inc., London/Prentice-Hall of Australia, Pty.
Ltd., Sydney/Prentice-Hall of Canada, Ltd., Toronto/Prentice-Hall of
India Private Ltd., New Delhi/Prentice-Hall of Japan, Inc., Tokyo/
Prentice-Hall of Southeast Asia Pte. Ltd., Singapore/Whitehall
Books Limited, Wellington, New Zealand
10   9   8   7   6   5   4   3   2

Library of Congress Cataloging in Publication Data

Peterson, Franklynn.
Children's toys you can build yourself.

Includes index.
1. Toy making—Amateurs' manuals.   I. Title.
TT174.P47   745.59'2   77-28948
ISBN 0-13-132613-9
ISBN 0-13-132506-X pbk

Dedicated to my very special playmate,
Judi, who turned life back into a playroom
full of exotic and quixotic delights.

Introduction

The message of this book is that *anyone* can do the things Franklynn Peterson has demonstrated. It doesn't matter if you start making a boat and it comes out looking like a house. The *real* message behind this message is that parents who may have a communication problem now have a new way of relating or "talking" to their children.

Many adults feel more comfortable talking to a child "through" an object. As a doctor, I am supposed to be an expert in looking people in the eye and getting them to believe what I know to be life's truths. As a parent, I often found it difficult being face-to-face with any of my own children. But if I could read a poem or story to them, or help my child with math, or Latin, or go on a nature hike, or help him pound a nail, I was "telling" that child that I was interested in him/her as a person. I was using my time to show that I had accepted that child as a part of my environment. I *cared*—and in a real, palpable way. This book offers one way to achieve that valuable parent-child relationship.

In the old days, fathers taught their sons how to farm, fish, or hunt. Mothers taught their daughters how to cook, sew, and care for babies. That's all considered sexist now. But the modern separation of parents and children is lamentable. Usually we parents find that most communication with our offspring is in the form of questions or commands. "What are you doing now?" "Go to bed." "Don't forget to brush your teeth." A child interprets these as put-downs; an indication that we consider him immature and in need of constant supervision. (Do you remember the last time your mother asked if you had on your clean underwear—even if you were 18 years old?) Children do not think as we adults do, but they feel just as acutely about put-downs, slights, or other evidence of rejection. They begin to wonder, "Why am I here? I can't do anything right." They need to feel acceptance. They see through the off-handed, "Sure, we love you, but get out of here."

It is well known that parents who are verbally facile are less likely to use physical punishment in disciplining their children. And, as a general rule, people who are more physical than verbal are more likely to be more strict and physical in their control of their children's behavior. It may also follow that people who can do things with their hands may be able to show, by example, the fun of making things. Although they are familiar with the technique of home toy manufacture, they need to have this book to realize the importance of this form of interaction with their children.

But the best use of this book will be in the homes where the parents are more verbal, or love to read, or are spectator types who just sit and watch TV. This book might be just the thing for a rather maladroit parent to get a child—boy or girl—to do something manually. Stamp collecting is okay. Learning cooking skills is valuable. Music lessons may be a drag to some children. But the mutual carpentry of parent and child can be one of the most valuable learning and maturing experiences a child can have.

Children want to love and respect their parents, and vice versa. We want to be proud of them. We want them to accomplish something, anything, so we can give them a few positive strokes. Now Peterson encourages us out of this pejorative habit of bad-mouthing our children. He allows us a chance to say something positive about them. Children really want to be at least accepted, if not loved,

for something they can do, besides just being cute. And if they can put a toy together themselves and some adult says, "Hey, that's great!" their self-esteem inches up a few points.

If you can read—and even if you can't—you can put a toy together. If parents have the techniques and the material and will set aside the time, the rest should be easy. Therefore, mother or father, turn off the TV and begin to bang a nail into a board, or cut a picture frame, or make a box. Sing or whistle while you bang around. A reasonably normal, perceptive child cannot help but be curious. The nice thing about children is that they don't *really* care if the box, game, car, or house is a perfect scale model or a shining and smooth replica of what they see on TV; they are cheered by the fact that it is something special for them. Once you get him/her close, say you are tired and ask, "Would you saw for a while?" You've got the child hooked.

Peterson has done for children's crafts what Rhoda Kellogg has done for children's art. She advises us to comment on the child's expression of the world as that particular child perceives it. Do not ask, "What the devil is that?" or "What an odd dog!" but say, "Tell me about the picture," or "I like the way you capture the essence of dogginess." Thus, when your child gets something done at the workbench, you say, "Tell me about this." You then smile and look him/her in the eyes and get interested. You may have to *act* a little, because the creative imagination you had when you were this child's age has been atrophied by education and making a living.

I remember my father helping me with a dog house

for our dog. I wasn't doing too well by myself, and he began to "help" more and more with, "Here, let me show you how to nail that," and "Put the shingles on like this." Please parents, let him/her do it alone. Interfere only just before tears of frustration begin to flow. And don't attempt any of this on an empty stomach; low blood sugar allows hammers to pound thumbs and saws to cut fingers. It may even be best to leave a little something for the next day.

The whole point of all this is that toy-making and playing have to be *fun*. But the odd thing you will notice is that you will become wrapped up in your child's enthusiasm. One look at the child's face when you say, "What thing in this book would you like to make?" and you will know *you* are hooked, too. You may have to control yourself or you will start making everything in this book yourself in hopes that your child will say something nice about *you*. But why not give it a try? Maybe your child will be able to make a splint for your smashed finger, at least.

—Lendon H. Smith, M.D.

Contents

1 I'm just mad about toys

I recently spent a few days in New York at the annual Toy Fair, where manufacturers hard-sell their latest offerings to toy-store buyers. There are 1,000 or so toymakers in the $6-billion-a-year toy industry. Among them, they grind out 150,000 different toys. And out of that bunch, there are at least 149,995 I wouldn't give my kids.

At the Fair I found out that one of the nation's largest manufacturers of "educational" toys had been swallowed by a conglomerate, and their line of toys had changed, perhaps to reflect a bigger profit margin. Their sturdy blackboard-and-painting-easel with four legs and an over-sized paint-catching tray, had suddenly lost half its legs and three quarters of its roomy tray. They had also switched from sensuous, fun-to-hold wooden cars and buses to plastic imitations disguised to look vaguely like wood. It's the same kind of trick that food processors play on grownups when they spray artificial coloring on oranges.

Also at the Toy Fair I saw a plastic something that slightly resembled a chicken. Fortunately a sign in front of it said "Chicken." It was advertised as "a wonderful educational toy to teach kids numbers and simple addition." I pushed the chicken's buttons, numbered 1, 2, and 3—and discovered that they had nothing at all to do with numbers or addition. Push a "1" and a baby chick appears in Mommy Chicken's tummy. Push "1" six times and six chicks pop into the tummy. Aside from the fact that chicks don't come from pushing buttons, and they neither start nor end up inside a chicken's tummy, the toy's not doing badly yet. You get one chick every time you push the "1" button.

But what happens if you push the button labeled "2"? Do you get two chicks? Nope! Instead, "2" makes Mommy

Figure I-1. These unimaginative, relatively rigid baseball players are typical of the "educational" playthings stocked by most toy stores

Chicken's giant plastic belly button flash a number equal to the number of little darlings you've put into her belly. And what's "3" for? Push it and the chicks vanish so the confused little child can start the "educational" process all over again.

In the display of a major "educational" craft and science toymaker I looked at expensively priced sets of tools that were cheaply built. Imagine some parent handing Junior or Sis a set of tools from this brand-name company and saying, "Now you're ready to start making things like grownups"—and then seeing that the wood that came with the tools was so thin and flaky it splintered and chipped when sawed with the barely sharp saw included in the kit. And imagine the disillusionment of a youngster who has trouble holding on to the too-small nails or discovers that the do-it-yourself section of that kit includes a tube with no more than *exactly* the number of nails required for the accompanying projects! In the same kit the cheaply built hammer head had been given a coating to make it look better. But the coating was so poorly applied it would certainly chip as soon as a youngster used it, and that chip could easily end up in the child's eye.

A prize-winning toymaker has put together a free "consumer guide" that, according to its public relations department, "stresses the importance of buying a toy that is fun as well as educational." That company's most highly advertised "educational" toy is called "Super Jock." It *teaches* that if you hit the garish-looking pitcher on the head, he pitches a ball at the grotesque-looking batter, who will swing if you hit *him* hard enough on the head.

Toys can *all* be educational if they expose a growing

child to new experiences, new faces, new objects, new colors, new shapes, or new forms of socialization.

Dr. Peter H. Wolff and Dr. Richard I. Feinbloom, two Boston pediatricians and professors at Harvard Medical School, found themselves besieged by parents concerned over whether they had chosen the right "educational" toys. When the doctors studied all the scientific journals on the subject, they could find no evidence whatsoever that toys are even necessary for normal child development. In their article in the medical journal *Pediatrics,* they stated that they considered it highly unethical for toy companies, not to mention doctors, professors, or educators, to claim that toys in themselves have educational value.

H. Robert Quilitch, director of the department of psychology at Nevada Mental Health Institute, also became curious about the toymakers' claims that their products were educational. Together with a colleague, Bob invested in a supply of "educational" $16 toy clocks touted as responding "to your child's desire to learn to tell time—all by himself." In a test, Quilitch found that first-graders who had the expensive clocks didn't learn how to tell time any faster than the kids who didn't. Testing third-graders, he found that students with the costly toy learned just slightly faster. *However,* if their parents showed them how a real $5 clock works, kids who didn't have the $16 toy learned just as fast as those who did.

The toy industry knows that parents are starting to get mad about the choice of toys that's offered them. When *Toys,* an industry trade journal, surveyed families around the country, they found that parents wanted *safety* (99 percent checked "most important" or "important").

But instead of rushing back to its workshops to design safer and sturdier toys, the toy industry rushed to its typewriters to write glowing ad claims. One such press release reads:

"Where children are concerned, no industry can be too careful in the safe design of its products. This is certainly the case for the nation's toy industry, for only safe toys are fun for children." Later, it enumerates what the toy industry itself considers adequate workmanship. Here, in the industry's own words, are the tests that a toy truck must pass to get the industry's self-administered seal of approval:

"Drop test, specifying that the truck must be dropped *4 times* in various attitudes from a height of *3 feet* without cracking or breaking.

"Bending tests for wires and rods which require back and forth bending through a 120 degree arc for *30 bends* to test durability.

"Tumble test for wheeled toys requires that the toy must be tumbled down a flight of *6 steps* a total of *8 times* in various positions to determine durability and strength of construction." [Emphasis added.]

How many times would you expect your youngster to drop an average truck during its play life? If yours are like mine, they'll drop a truck 400 times, if it doesn't fall apart first!

Aside from their shoddy design and manufacture, there's another reason why so many toys fall apart so soon. When I was talking to Dr. Benjamin Spock, the famous baby doctor, he summed it up better than I might be able to. "A father buys his son a tin train," Ben said, "but the train isn't what the son wants. It's what the toy manufacturers think adults will buy. So the son soon takes the top off the passenger car in order to put blocks or marbles inside like a freight car. Or he takes the tin skin off the locomotive and turns it into a diesel because it looks different with the tin skin off. Children don't want to be cramped. They're naturally creative. It's the easiest thing in the world to encourage that creativity by giving them things with which they can make new things." How many toy trains that you've seen on toy-store shelves are as versatile as Ben Spock thinks they ought to be?

Giving children a mountain of toys, creative or otherwise, isn't a good idea either. Dr. Brian Sutton-Smith, Columbia University professor and developmental psychologist, is one of the few researchers in the area of toys. He's also a hired gun for the toy industry. Nevertheless, he told me, "Parents need to be selective. Presenting children with a confusing array of toys all at once may distract them and possibly diminish the satisfaction that is essential to happy and productive play."

He also agreed with Spock that, in the hands of alert parents, toys should help develop imagination. "The real secret to developing imaginative children lies in seeing other people acting imaginatively," Sutton-Smith said. "It's the actively involved, playful *parent*—assisted by toys and games—who determines how a child's imagination will develop."

We and our children can start taking charge of toys, games, and playthings. We can stop spending outrageous sums of money for gauchely colored bits of fragile plastic that aren't half as much fun as a 5-minute romp with Mom or Pop. We can start to make toys for and with our children; to their tastes and ours, for their individual interests and our own.

Start by reading all the way through this book. See what intrigues you. Ask your children—the ones who are old enough to understand pictures—which toys most appeal to them. Pick out a project that matches your skills. If you're a rank beginner, find one with an easy skills rating. But by the time you've built a couple of the easier projects, you will be skillful enough to make every toy in this book.

Not every child moves along the path toward adulthood at the same rate. You have to be the ultimate judge of which toys are suited for which children, and when. To help you make a general selection, though, I've rated each toy according to a chart initially developed by Dr. Sutton-Smith that details what skills the educational/psychological community believes that children experiment with at particular ages.

Just as I hope you don't listen to everything the TV or the toy industry tells you about toys, I hope you won't follow my suggestions indiscriminately. After all, at the tender age of 39, I'm still in my first childhood. If I recommend a natural-wood finish, finish it that way if you prefer—or paint it as bright as you want. If I show how to make a 12-inch-long bus, but you want a super-bus, 48 inches long—well, just build the darn thing.

2 *Tools of the toy trade*

(For children 3 years and up)

Obviously you can't build toys without tools. But what isn't so obvious is that kids can make great use of tools as toys. I'm not talking about toys that look like tiny tools and *almost* cut wood. I'm talking about real tools you can buy at your local hardware store.

When they're about 5 years old, most children can handle a selection of real tools. I bought David a set of tools for his fifth birthday. We built the toolbox together, using his own tools, and he hasn't hurt himself seriously or gotten into trouble with his tools from the first day he opened the present.

Most adults think it's preposterous to give saws and hammers to kids. Grown-ups are afraid the children will hurt themselves, and badly. But if children have trouble working with tools of any sort, it's because *nobody ever showed them how*. There are only a few elementary woodworking techniques, and they can be set down in the space of a few pages. You'll be able to apply them to just about *every* project in this book. You can show them to your children, or better still, you can learn them *along* with your children. Youngsters get a real sense of participation if they can learn something at the same time their parents or teachers are learning it.

Even if you're well experienced in the use of tools, the following material represents some of the safest and surest methods—the ones that children should learn.

Dr. Rose Mukerji, professor of early childhood education at Brooklyn College, is one of the most respected people in the field of child's play. I spent a

Figure II-1. With "tool" sets like these, it's hard for a child to realize the fun of building things properly. And too often, the contents are poorly assembled and impractical

morning with her recently to find out what she's learned about toys and tools in her decades of research and teaching. She told me, "Tools, like musical instruments and similar devices, serve a child's own purposes beautifully. They give the child a sense of control, and that's an important aspect in play."

Rose has children as young as three using tools in preschool programs at the Brooklyn College developmental labs. She suggests that how soon you should introduce a set of tools depends on whether you want to supervise their use for the first few months after you buy them. If you plan to get actively involved in helping your children use tools, then you can introduce the hammers, saws, and such much earlier. But with most children, some advice in how to work with tools is important at the outset.

From her years of experience, Dr. Mukerji drew up a list of approximate ages she's found most suited to start using various tools. These are just guidelines. Your children may be ready for some tools sooner; others may have to wait awhile.

Saw, hammer, drills, and sandpaper at age 3. Girls, being better coordinated as a rule, can start sooner than boys.

Square, pencil, file, and SurForm tool at age 4.

Screwdriver with bolts at age 7.

Coping saw at age 9 or 10.

The tools themselves don't have to be expensive, but you should buy them at a hardware store and not a dime store. Some of the cheapie imports are OK, but so many of them aren't that it's not worth taking a chance unless you can recognize good tools from the bad.

Here's a list of beginning tools which should go into your child's first tool set:

Vise (small tabletop model)
C-clamps (two 6″ size)
Saw (12″ to 16″ blade)
Coping saw (with half a dozen extra blades)
Hammer (full-size, but lightweight)
Square
Pencil
Brace
Bits (¼″, ½″, 1″)
SurForm tool (small, scraper or plane model)
Assorted sandpaper
Screwdriver
Pliers

You should also buy some hardware when you buy the tools. Here's a good start:

Common or box nails—2d (about 1″ long)—one-pound box
Common or box nails—6d (about 2″ long)—one-pound box
Bolts and nuts—¼″ x 2″—small plastic box

A *vise* fastens temporarily, via a small thumbscrew, to a desk or tabletop. With a larger thumbscrew, you can clamp a board or other large object into the jaws of the vise. That holds the work steady. Without a vise, children under about 8 or 9 years old cannot work successfully with most tools.

Figure II-2. David's set of basic tools from the hardware store and the toolbox he and I built together

C-clamps work like a vise, but are easy to carry around. You and the children can use C-clamps to hold on to odd-shaped projects. Also, in case you have a long board in the vise and want to hold another long piece atop it, use a C-clamp.

Common wood saws manufactured for use by adults are too large for children. They're overly large for a few grown-up beginners, too. Find one with a blade from 12" to 18" long. Most often you'll settle on a saw featuring interchangeable blades. Frankly, most of the non-standard blades are of only very limited use, so don't buy a saw based solely on how many different kinds of blades come with it.

When you saw, you should always have a pencil line to follow. To begin the cut, set the saw carefully on the pencil line at the edge of your board. If you're right-handed, hold the saw in place with your left thumb. With your right hand, slowly pull and push the saw until it cuts deeply enough into the wood to support itself. Then you can withdraw your thumb and begin making more and more vigorous strokes. Use as much of the blade as possible, not only the few inches near the middle. When the saw is close to the end of its cut, you have to resume the slower, shorter strokes. If you hold on to the loose part of your board at this stage of sawing, you will end up with a smooth, squared-off job. Otherwise the final ½" may chip off precipitously.

A *coping saw* is useful for cutting circular patterns and holes. Its very thin blade saws around even very tight curves. If you want to cut in the middle of a piece of wood, drill a small hole where the cut will go. Slip your coping saw

blade out of its handle, fit the blade into the hole, reattach the handle, and then make your cuts.

You can also cut thin or very soft metal and plastic with a coping saw. For that you need blades designed for metal cutting. Buy plenty of inexpensive extra blades, because they snap rather easily (but I've never seen anybody hurt by a snapping blade).

Don't buy a tiny *hammer*. Since you and the children will be working on full-size nails, the hammer, too, should be full size. But hammers come in varying weights. Buy one of the lightest you can find—well under a pound. Avoid hammer heads that have been given a coating of shiny metal, which can flake or chip off and fly into somebody's eye. Besides, the metal plating is probably an indication of very inferior metal underneath.

A *square* is often overlooked when people are buying tools. It won't be the cheapest tool on your list, but it's important. If you plan to saw two pieces of wood and then fasten them together, they'll fit much better if the sawed ends are cut at fairly precise right angles. With a small square, you can draw accurately placed lines.

Most squares have a ruler included. Look for one at least 8 inches long. A 10" or 12" ruler is better, but also more expensive. Don't forget to include a pencil for drawing lines.

The *brace and bits* drills holes in wood, but for some reason this poor misnamed tool is never called a "wood drill." The handle is called the *brace* and the spiraled "drills" are the *bits*. Bits come in various sizes and styles for cutting smooth holes up to 2" or 3" in diameter.

The squared end of the bit slips into the brace's

opening. When you twist its metal opening clockwise, the jaws close firmly around the bit, a skill which 7- or 8-year-olds can acquire with a bit of coaching.

There's a screw-shaped tip to most bits that bores into the wood in the center where you want the hole cut. It pulls the bit's blade into the wood to slice away spiral layer after layer of wood. If you go all the way through the wood in one operation, you'll probably knock some chips loose, resulting in a messy-looking hole. Instead, when the screw tip pokes through the bottom of your wood, stop. Turn the brace counterclockwise to pull the bit out of the hole. Flip over the wood and start the bit into the hole from the opposite direction.

The *SurForm tool* is a relatively recent invention. Its roughened blade smoothly rubs away controllable amounts of wood. You can use it to smooth off rough edges or to impart a new shape to flat wood. For instance, if you repeatedly run a flat or gently curved SurForm tool along the squared edge of a board, you can round it off. On the other hand, when you get boards from a lumberyard, they're often rough along their edges. With a SurForm tool, you can remove the roughness but keep the edges flat if you hold the tool flat.

Sandpaper should be treated as a tool even though it's disposable. It comes in all kinds of roughness grades ranging from very coarse to superfine. It is used to smooth wood surfaces until defects no longer mar the beauty of the wood. You'll be using lots of wood in these toys, and you'll want it to come out looking as smooth and beautiful as possible.

You won't have a lot of use for coarse sandpaper in toy making, but the kids will enjoy seeing what the different sandpaper surfaces can do. For most wood projects, I start with fine sandpaper. If you or the kids have dented and knicked the wood, you might prefer to start sanding with medium grade and then switch to fine. For some projects you may want to employ extra-fine-grade sandpaper. The only way you'll know is to buy a sheet and try it.

Most sandpaper comes in 9″ by 12″ sheets, which are much too large to be useful. Cut or tear them into quarters. The edge of your saw makes a fine tool for tearing sandpaper. You'd be surprised how dull your scissors would become after cutting just a few sheets of it.

For sanding flat surfaces, wrap your quarter sheet of sandpaper around a small piece of scrap lumber or a blackboard eraser. Otherwise your fingers or hand will press unevenly and result in uneven spots on your wood. But do use your fingers to fit sandpaper into holes, grooves, curves, and other irregular pieces of wood.

A screwdriver is needed for several reasons. Most of all, it helps your kids know they've got a real set of tools. They see screwdrivers in use fixing TVs, washing machines, cars, and other popular items. If they own one too, it helps them believe that they're big-time builders.

Since Junior may want to bolt wheels or levers onto his creations, bolts are included in my hardware shopping list. Stop at the bolt counter first. Then find a screwdriver which has a tip that just fits into the bolt head's slot. That way the screwdriver is less likely to slip when Junior bolts his projects together.

A pliers, like the screwdriver, is a prestige tool. A kid has to have one to feel "with it." And it's useful when Sis starts to turn bolts tightly with her screwdriver. She can use the pliers to hold on to the nut at the other end.

Nails hold most children's own projects together. For the toys we'll build, we'll almost always use nails where they can be hidden. We'll choose finishing nails or brads (the terms mean almost the same thing); they have tiny heads that are easy to conceal. Other fastening devices—screws, bolts, pegs, and so on—are a bit tough for younger children and many adults.

Ideally, a nail should be almost twice as long as the width of the board it's holding. That means Junior will have to pound a bit to get his birdhouses and bridges fastened together. You might be tempted to buy shorter nails so he can fasten more with less pounding. But you'll only frustrate him in the end, because the too-short nails will come loose, the project will fall apart, and Junior's likely to feel his creation's a flop. So let him pound. He could be pounding on worse things than nails.

For kids, I've included only common nails on the shopping list. Those are the relatively thick nails with the big heads that make good-sized targets for hammers in small hands. The big heads also make bent nails easier to pull out.

Here's how you can show a daughter or son a safe but effective way to hammer nails. Hold the nail very straight with thumb and index finger. Then tap it gently with a hammer. When the point is deep enough that the nail can stand alone, pull your fingers out of the way. Tap a little harder with the hammer until you're sure the nail is going in correctly. Then you can hit the nail hard as long as the impact doesn't make the nail go crooked.

If the nail starts going crooked, stop. Tap it gently on the side to straighten it out. Then tap lightly on top until it's moving straight into the wood again.

Children often intuitively hold a hammer the right way. They grab it near the end, especially when they're hitting hard. That's great! Don't try to correct them. I've seen parents try to convince a child she should hold the hammer near its head, thinking incorrectly that it's safer that way. It isn't!

A *toolbox* is the first thing you and the kids should build together once you've assembled the tools. The message has to be made very clear that a set of tools (like many other toys) isn't useful unless the full set is kept intact and in good working condition. A toolbox makes sure that all the pieces will be stored in one place, can be carried easily to a "job site," and won't become hazards if a sharp bit is laid on a bed or a handful of nails is scattered across the playroom floor.

Figures II-3 through II-5 show how to construct a simple but effective toolbox. The exact length of the box depends on your saw's length. The dimensions shown presume that your saw is no longer than 15″. If your saw exceeds that, you have to lengthen boards C, D, and E plus dowel F just enough so the saw will fit snugly into the toolbox.

With the dimensions shown here, you can go to a lumberyard and ask for a 1 x 8″ (read "one by eight inch") pine board 6′ long. Ask for "sterling" grade of lumber. If you need a longer toolbox, you'll have to buy a piece 8′ long, since they generally come only in even-numbered lengths. You'll need one piece of ½″ dowel for the handle.

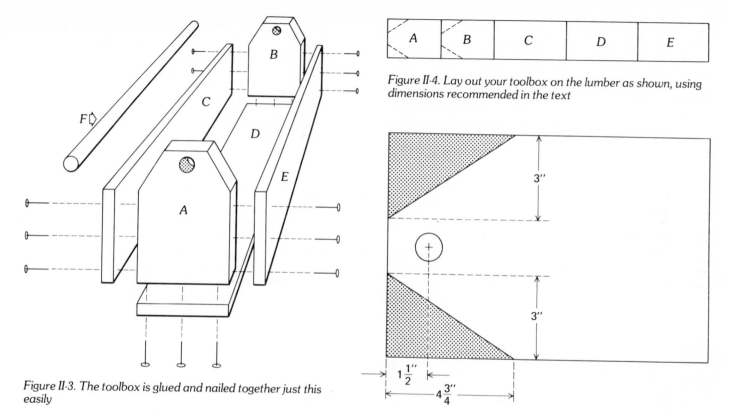

Figure II-3. The toolbox is glued and nailed together just this easily

A	B	C	D	E

Figure II-4. Lay out your toolbox on the lumber as shown, using dimensions recommended in the text

3″

3″

$1\frac{1}{2}″$

$4\frac{3}{4}″$

Figure II-5. Pattern for ends of toolbox (A and B)

All of the materials for this toolbox will cost you less than the price of meat for one family meal.

Measure the end pieces (A and B) onto your board. Then saw them out along with the other pieces. Nail them together (using 2″ brads) according to Figure II-3. First nail the bottom (C) to the ends (A and B). Nail the sides (D and E) on next. Slip the dowel (F) into its hole.

Anything that gets as much use as this toolbox probably should be fastened together with glue as well as nails. A common general-purpose product such as Elmer's Glue-All is plenty strong enough for projects you'll be working on in this book. If for some reason you decide not to use glue, fasten the dowel into place with a nail through the end boards (A and B) at each extremity.

Sharp kids may ask why the adults use glue on the toolbox when they can't use glue on their own projects. My answer has been, "Glue is important for a project like this, that will get hard use and has to last a long time. You may want to make a change in the toys you'll be constructing and glue would make that almost impossible. Besides, glue gets out of the bottle too easily and messes up tables, clothes, hands, and floors. You know what happens when you make that kind of mess! So let's wait and use glue when you're older."

Wood for the woodworker's projects doesn't have to be expensive. Lumberyards often have a scrap pile for excess and odd-shaped pieces of boards. Most yards are delighted when somebody volunteers to carry away some of the scrap.

Even if you have to buy new lumber for children's projects, the cost is modest. You can cut up the long boards into kid-sized pieces, or you can ask the lumberyard to do it for you. Here's one basic pile you might want to use for a starter. Buy two boards, each 8′ long, one 1″ x 4″ and one 1″ x 2″. From each board, cut up:

> five pieces at 4″
> six pieces at 6″
> five pieces at 8″

I'd also buy a few ½″ dowels and cut them up into a mixture of pieces 2″, 4″, 6″, and 8″ long.

Don't stop with wood. Junior builders can put plenty of other common materials to good use when they improvise a castle, train, supermarket, barn, or airport. Ordinary cardboard boxes, for instance, can be cut into "boards" that cover a lot of ground and are extremely easy to nail into place. Here's a list of some other "building materials" I've found handy:

> Baking powder cans
> Styrofoam packing (although a bit messy at times)
> Round oatmeal and salt boxes
> Jar covers
> Plastic food containers
> Cigar boxes

Playing with tools, children can build some of the toy projects from this book. Or they can design and build their own cities, buildings, vehicles, people, animals, or things not yet known to science. Keeping in mind that a toy that teaches can also be fun, *let* the tools be fun, and put as few regulations as possible on their use.

Don't insist that *every* project Sis starts has to be finished. Maybe the design looks finished to her long before it looks finished to you. On the other hand, if you get the idea that she's leaving lots of her handywork unfinished because she doesn't know how to carry it further, you might say, "Hey, that's a great beginning. I think it would look super if we *tried to* put wheels on." Try not to assume that you can do something David or Kevin can't. If they're stuck, offer to give the problem a try, which is what you'd like them to do when they're up against a problem—try.

Don't insist that Junior build realistic-looking cars, people, buildings, or anything else. What may look too simple and undetailed to an adult looks real through a child's eyes. I'd like to see adults stop "teaching" children that each drawing or craft project needs to have every hair copied on before it's finished. Picasso, I understand, once remarked that it took him years and years before he relearned to see the world like a child. That should make us all stop and think before we insist that Sis's airplane have a visible propellor or jet engines, or Junior's house have a visible roof.

3 *Blocks, blocks, blocks*

(6 months to 10 years old)

A castle, touching lofty clouds, where eagles pause for a breath of fragrant air. A McDonald's where twenty-seven juicy Big Macs a minute bounce off a computerized assembly line and pop right into customers' expectant mouths. An easy chair that shuts out unpleasant noises and scoldings. All that and more—from blocks.

Over a glass of beer one day, Dr. Spock told me what wonderful all-purpose, highly creative toys he thought blocks can be. "From the age of one until at least twelve,"

Figure III-1. Though Oscar's set of blocks consists of Con-Tact plastic over old boxes, it's just as colorful as any set on sale downtown

he said, "my two sons were using their blocks *at least half the time they were playing.*"

The famed pediatrician and author lamented, "To many parents, blocks don't seem dramatic enough. They'd rather buy a tin soccer game or a tin football game or tin trains. But with blocks, the child *can make* all these things. And he makes something different *every* day he plays with them. Very few families have blocks in large numbers, even though they're standard in a nursery school or child development center. They're fairly expensive, but infinitely worthwhile."

By now you've probably forgotten all the wondrous things you built from blocks in your own childhood. And they needn't have been elaborate sets. Mine were wooden cubes less than two inches on a side, on which some clever manufacturer had painted cows, horses, and the alphabet.

Today you can spend a handsome sum of money on a really gorgeous set of blocks. If you have the money, by all means buy them. But you can build your own blocks, involve your children in the building, and save a great deal of money. And your homemade blocks will be very personal, doubly inspiring playthings.

HOLLOW BLOCKS

(6 months to 5 years to play with; 8 years and up to build.)
Skills: Extremely easy.
Materials: Several yards of self-adhesive vinyl plastic. Miscellaneous empty boxes.

Hollow blocks are great for younger children. They're lightweight, colorful, and versatile. But when you want to make a set of blocks like these, it pays to plan ahead. The materials are empty household containers and tubes, and you'll want to save lots of them. Like that old Cracker Jack slogan, the more you make, the more you'll want. Maybe the neighbors will help by saving up tubes and containers such as these:

　　Baking powder cans
　　Baking soda boxes
　　Cheese boxes
　　Salt boxes
　　Oatmeal boxes
　　Cocoa boxes
　　Toilet tissue tubes
　　Paper towel tubes
　　Aluminum foil tubes

　　Jewelry boxes
　　Book mailers
　　Breadcrumb boxes
　　Peanut cans
　　Coffee cans
　　Spice boxes
　　Pancake mix boxes

All of these, plus any other reasonably rugged containers, can be converted into a wonderful set of blocks.

You can use milk cartons, both one-quart and two-quart sizes. Even the pint and half-pint sizes are OK. Wash them out well and let them dry thoroughly. Before they work as blocks, you have to punch down that peak where the milk pours out. It's relatively easy to square off that end. When the old milk carton gets covered with a new skin of colorful Con-Tact vinyl plastic (or a similar product), like magic it becomes a large block. The Con-Tact plastic adds more than just color—it helps strengthen the container enormously.

When you wrap your milk carton in vinyl, make sure to stretch the plastic tightly. Milk containers have a habit of bulging in the middle. If you don't break that habit with a good stiff application of self-adhesive plastic plus elbow grease, the blocks won't stack well on top of each other.

The major advantage of using milk containers is that they're easy to find. Most families with children use enough so you can save up a good-size set of blocks within a month. Milk containers are fine for very young children, but they're quite lightweight, and not as rugged as some other containers. By the time children reach the turbulent threes, they will probably need something more heavy-duty.

When you buy self-adhesive vinyl, pick something colorful. If you choose a pattern, make sure the designs are small. If you want to work with solid colors, pick as many different colors as possible—red, white, green, yellow, black, orange, blue, silver, gold, purple—even though that's not as economical as covering the entire set of blocks from the same roll.

Wrap your blocks just the way you'd wrap a present. When you get to the round boxes and tubes, cover the round tops and bottoms first. Cut an over-size piece of vinyl, press it into place, and then slice the excess so it smooths neatly down onto the sides. When you cover the sides, your excess from the top is concealed.

Don't let the open ends of paper towel or toilet tissue tubes scare you. You can cover them with self-adhesive plastic just as if they had cardboard tops. But nobody says blocks *have to* look solid. If you like, you can cover the sides of your tubes with plastic and leave their ends wide open.

WOODEN BLOCKS

(2 to 10 years to play with; 4 years and up to help build.)
Skills: Easy.
Materials: Several hardwood or pine boards.

Wooden blocks are a delight for children of all ages, and a change from the glittery chrome and plastic environment we're building around ourselves. A full store-bought set is prohibitively expensive for most families. About the only places I've seen one is in school or in the playroom of a well-off friend. But for little money, you can *make* a set of those big natural-wood blocks.

This isn't an overnight project unless you have plenty of hands willing to pitch in. The reason wooden blocks are so expensive is that they require careful sanding. Even with sanding machines, the companies that build blocks have to pay the salaries of craftspeople to run wood through those machines. That's where the cost comes in. But you can sand by hand or with smaller sanding machines. Once you get the knack of sanding by hand, you don't even have to look. You can spend an evening watching TV and sanding blocks at the same time.

Hardwood such as maple is very nice for blocks. Oak, mahogany, birch, and other hardwoods work well too. If you can get the woods, you can even mix them up to give you a beautiful many-colored block set. But hardwoods are difficult to find in local lumberyards; even a large dealer rarely stocks much 2″ hardwood.

Pine is almost always available. In addition, it's cheaper, easier to sand, and looks just great. With a good grade of pine and a rugged finish, you won't encounter the problems of splintering and chipping.

Ask your lumberyard for their best grade of pine, which goes by various names: "number one" and "clear" are tops; "sterling" is right up there too. Try not to go down the quality ladder any further than that. Tell the lumberyard you want clean, dry, knot-free lumber even if you have to pay a bit extra for it. If they pull out some pieces you don't like, tell them to try again. It's your money, and you should be satisfied with the wood you're buying.

Here's the wood you should buy and the way to cut it

up to give you the raw materials for a basic set of wooden blocks:

> *1 piece 2″ x 4″, 8′ long:* 7 pieces @ 3½″; 4 pieces @ 7″; 4 pieces @ 10½″.
>
> *1 piece 1″ x 4″, 8′ long:* 5 pieces @ 3½″; 5 pieces @ 7″; 4 pieces @ 10½″.
>
> *1 piece closet pole 6′ long:* 9 pieces @ 1¾″; 12 pieces @ 3½″; 2 pieces @ 7″.
>
> *1 piece 1″ x 4″, 8′ long:* 7 pieces cut into 3½″ x 1¾″ arches; 8 pieces cut into 3½″ x 3½″ triangles; 6 pieces cut into 7″ x 3½″ triangles.

Figure III-3 presents graphically the simple process for laying out the arches and triangles onto your 1″ x 4″ board. The triangles are easy sawing jobs.

There are a couple of ways to cut the arches. The fastest makes use of a small electric drill. You can invest in a very inexpensive *hole cutter attachment* that makes holes larger than a brace and bit can easily tackle. Set your cutter for a hole close to 2″ in diameter. After you've marked the exact center of each appropriate 3½″ block, drill a 2″ hole. Then, when you saw the blocks in half, you'll have two arches.

A second method for cutting arches makes use of an electric sabre saw or a coping saw plus a regular handsaw. Using a compass or improvised tool, draw 2″ circles where the arches are supposed to go. Draw straight lines down the center of the joined seven pieces of 3½″ blocks that will soon be turned into arches. Saw along the dividing line

Figure III-2. A modest investment in wood can result in a set of blocks like this—versatile, lovely to look at, and worth $20 and up if bought in fancy toy stores

until you reach the first circle. Switch to a coping saw and cut out the circle. Then use your regular saw until you reach the second circle. A coping saw isn't often used to cut long straight lines because it's not easy to keep that tool going perfectly straight. (You can use a sabre saw for cutting both the curved and straight lines here.)

After you've cut up all of your lumber, you'll have ninety-four blocks in twelve different shapes and sizes. The lumber will cost you only 10 or 20 percent of a comparable set of factory-built blocks. That makes a few evenings of hand finishing very profitable.

Use a SurForm tool to smooth away all of the blocks' rough edges. In fact, if you find too many rough spots along entire sides of the long boards, you should use a SurForm tool (or electric sander) on them even before you take saw in hand.

Round off all square corners and edges with your SurForm tool. Round edges make these blocks safer, cutting down on the likelihood of splinters.

Sandpaper every block thoroughly. Begin with medium or fine, but always end up with nothing coarser than very fine. Every so often, dust off the block so you can see how you're doing. You'll know when the sanding is done—the wood's surface will look and feel like a baby's cheek.

Once sanded, the blocks are ready to play with—but I strongly recommend that you immediately protect and strengthen them with a wood finish. My choice is pene-trating wood sealer such as Fabulon's Polyurethane.

A quart of penetrating wood sealer should do for your entire set of blocks. This finish doesn't sit on the surface of wood like paint or varnish, but soaks in to seal the grain, harden the surface, and bring out a beautiful woodsy appearance. It makes wood look about as fine as any linseed oil or Danish oil can do. But you end up with a tougher finish, and it's faster than paint!

Don't bother to brush the sealer onto your blocks. With a pair of tongs, dip them one by one into the can. Set them on an inclined tray lined with wax paper. Any excess sealer will run off and you can pour it back into the can. It's wise, although not necessary, to turn over the blocks about half an hour after they're dipped. That way the side that rested on wax paper first will get a chance to shed excess sealer and dry. If you don't want to disturb your drying blocks, try to plunk the opposite end on the tray during the next dip.

Most of your sealer will soak in after the first dip. When it dries—in about half a day—dip again. You'll know when the wood has soaked up enough sealer because it will stop sinking in and start showing on the blocks' surface. When the dried blocks show a uniform sheen, that's enough sealer.

After you've finished the basic blocks, you might want to add to the set. Or the kids might order some custom-built blocks from you. You can simply duplicate

Figure III-3. Curved and triangular blocks are laid out on lumber in this fashion

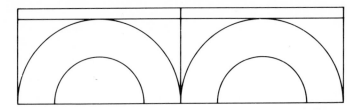

Figure III-4. Large arches are easily created this way

some of the instructions given earlier, or strike off on your own. Probably you'll have lots of ideas once you see a child start to play with them. That's one of the points of this book: to encourage you to play an active role in your children's play and education.

Let me share the rationale behind the dimensions used here. Even though the common or trade name for a board may be "1 by 4 inches," it really doesn't measure 1 by 4 inches at all. That was its size when it first passed through the sawmill. Later, planes ground away roughness caused by the saw, and sanders may have ground away coarseness caused by the planes. By the time a "1 x 4" reaches you, it's about ¾" thick and 3½" wide. A so-called "2 x 4" is closer to 1½" x 3½". But a board labeled "8" really is exactly 8′ in length, almost without exception.

I had to keep those board sizes in mind when I sat down to sketch out a set of blocks. I wanted them to fit together, so the blocks' length had to relate to their width. Consequently, the length of most of the blocks is a multiple of the width, 3½" (3½, 7, 10½). If you want to add some really long blocks to this set, you might want to stick with multiples of 3½" such as 14, 17½, or 21. But by the time Junior puts a long block into some project, he's probably used a few other blocks sideways, so uniformity becomes less important in longer sizes.

There are plenty of other shapes you can add to your blocks, too. First off, I like to see simple cylinders or small squares in odd sizes. We're left with a few of them after cutting up the basic block set described earlier. Some ¾" and 1" pieces, either from flat boards or the round closet poles, help to shore up all kinds of projects that come out only close to right on the first try.

A couple of variations in the arches can be fun. You can cut some out of either 1″ x 8″ or 2″ x 8″ boards. I'd recommend the 2″ boards if you can get good quality lumber in that size and can get hold of a sabre saw. It isn't always easy hand-sawing through the thicker board, but it can be done with a coping saw and persistence. If you simply sketch the arches from Figure III-4 onto the 8″ lumber, you'll have double-sized arches for your block collection.

You can toss spindle spacers or whole spindles into the block box, or you can cut sundry sizes of spindle pieces. Open up your mind a bit to let through some input from your child. I can still remember when David made his own set of blocks by literally ripping apart an aging coffee table I once built out of hardwood. He was only two when he started the project, three by the time he had all twenty-four of the simple hardwood blocks pried loose. He's played with them for more hours than with any other single toy. And they still fit with most of the highways and buildings he makes with more expensive, more sophisticated toys!

4 *A moving set of toys*

(1 to 10 years to play with; 8 to 16 years to build.)
Skills: Not difficult, but some patience required.

In any toy display, those beautiful, simple-looking, wooden, wheeled, and expensive cars, trucks, trains, and planes are usually the highlight. They're as much fun to build as they are to use.

When I showed the early sketches for these movable toys to Rose Mukerji, the Brooklyn College professor of early childhood education, her face lit up. "Oh, they're just lovely!" she cried. "They make you want to just reach out and handle them. Wood is so much fun to hold."

Look back into the last chapter for a review of which

Figure IV-1. Kevin's oak bus and David's mahogany sportscar that he helped design (the spare tire was David's idea)

wood works best for blocks. The same advice applies here. Even the finishing is the same, except that you may want to use a paintbrush to apply the sealer instead of dipping toys directly into the can.

Most of these are built around a 2″ x 4″ board. On some of them, a piece or two of 1″ x 4″ board is added. For the locomotive, you need a short piece of closet pole, a wooden rod generally between 1½″ and 2″ in diameter. Short dowels, ¼″, ½″ and 1″ fit into a few projects. Wheels can be sliced from closet poles, or you can buy ready-made spacers in the spindle section of your hardware or lumber store. (More on that later.)

Tools are simple, too. You'll need a handsaw (although sabre saws are fine) plus a brace and bit. The three bit sizes listed in the tool chapter are more than enough. Also, you have to round many edges on these toys. You can use a coping saw (or sabre saw) to establish the basic curves, then a SurForm tool to round the edges further, and finally medium-grade sandpaper to smooth down your wood all the way. Alternatively, you can use a handsaw to cut on the straight lines plus make straight cuts close to curved lines, and then use a SurForm tool to create curves. Ironically, I think the two methods consume about the same amount of time and energy.

Layout drawings nearby show all the shapes and measurements you need. You can draw the proper shape onto your 2″ x 4″ board in two ways. One is to use a ruler to measure and mark off all the straight lines. Then use a compass to draw the quarter- and half-circle curves. The layout drawings show the radius of curves. For example, the *1″R* next to the curved hood of the little car in Figure IV-3 shows you that the radius is 1″. So set the legs of your compass 1″ apart to draw the hood curve. (If you don't have a compass handy, improvise with a nail and piece of string.)

There's another way you can draw toy shapes onto wood. Use a ruler to mark ½″ squares on the wood. Then copy the drawings from this book onto the squares on your wood, proceeding square by square. You don't have to copy the circles that represent windows on the car and other toys. Just mark where the center of each circle will go. When you bore each hole with your brace and bit, place the tip of the bit on the center mark.

JUST A CAR

First, cut off a 6″ piece of 2″ x 4″ board. Then draw the shape onto it. Using coping saw or sabre saw, cut out the basic wooden car shape. Next put a 1″ bit into your brace and bore the two window holes.

After that, use a SurForm tool to really round off every edge and corner. Follow up with medium-grade sandpaper to smooth off the curves some more. Then you can sand the toy with fine and perhaps even very fine sandpaper until the surfaces glisten. Don't forget to sandpaper at least a bit inside the holes. To accomplish that, roll a small piece of sandpaper around one finger.

WHEELS

Wheels for all these toys can be slices of closet pole, each ¾″ thick. Round off both the inside and outside edges until the outer surface of each looks like a round tire. The wheels are held on to your cars and trucks with ¼″ by 1¼″ *lag screws,* which good hardware stores stock.

Bore a ¼″ hole through the exact center of each wheel. Slip your lag screw into the hole and screw it into an appropriate place on your toy. If you're working with pine, you can probably get the screw started without much trouble. If you're using hardwood, or if you have trouble with pine, mark the spot where each wheel should go and make a small hole with a hammer and nail, electric drill, or similar gadget. The absolute best way is to drill a ³⁄₁₆″ hole into the car, smear the end of the lag screw with wax or hand soap, and then twist in the screw the proper distance with a good wrench. A pliers is your next-best choice.

Lazy folks like a different approach. If you're one of us, go out and buy some *spacers* in the spindle section of your favorite lumber or hardware store. They're shaped like tires and have a hole in the middle. The variety I prefer

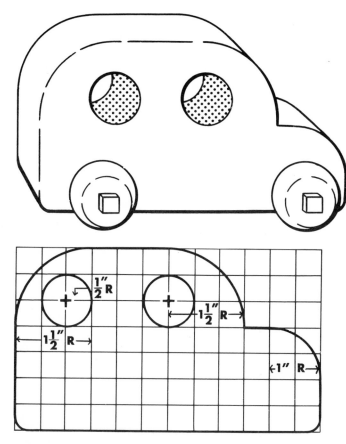

Figure IV-2-3. Simple but imagination-provoking car you can build from hard or soft wood—or better yet, let the kids construct. Lay out your car on lumber via ½-inch squares sketched onto a pattern paper, or directly onto the wood

(which incidentally is the least expensive, too) has a hole just right for the ¼″ lag screws I recommend.

It's impossible to show on our layout drawings exactly where the wheels should go because the diameters of closet poles and spacers vary. You should try to start the point of your lag screw at least ⅜″ from the bottom of the toy. If you move it closer to the edge, you risk splitting the wood.

Some readers may have doubts about the wisdom of using large screws in children's toys. But here's why: One common method of fastening wheels to some of the expensive so-called educational toys is by using very narrow wooden dowels. The idea is that the toy will be safe if everything is made out of wood. Problem is, thin wooden dowels break rather easily, and when they do, there are generally some sharp edges and splinters.

Another common method for holding wheels on to commercially produced toys is with small nails or screws. The federal standard for toy trucks requires only that wheels on some toys withstand a 10-pound pressure. Older children can pry nails loose and younger children can hammer them loose. Screws are harder to extract, but the threads on smaller screws will loosen if the wood around them starts to dry up.

That's why I've opted for very large screws. The threads are so big that I've never known one to work loose due to drying lumber. And I've suspended all 185 pounds of me from the wheel on one of these toys—between ten and twenty times more than the federal standard requires—and haven't compromised the screw. As you'll see when you have to reach for a wrench or pliers to twist a ¼″ lag screw into wood, it won't be easy for children to loosen one.

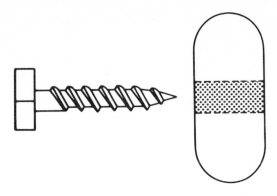

Figure IV-4. Cross section of safe but rugged wheels for these vehicles

I rather enjoy the look of screw heads on the wheels—they're almost like hubcaps. But if you find them offensive, bore a shallow hole (¼" to ⅜" deep) on the outside of each wheel with your ½" bit. The lag screw will slip into the hole and be less conspicuous. To hide it altogether, glue a thin slice of wood from a closet pole over it.

BUS

The bus is built exactly like the car, only in my drawings it's twice as long. If you want a shorter bus—or you have a shorter piece of wood on hand—make it a little shorter. These toys belong to you and your kids.

SPORTSCAR

Our sportscar uses the 2" x 4" board sideways. The other toy designs here generally use the 4" edge for the side of a bus, car, airplane, or train. This sporty convertible uses the 2" edge for its side. Drill two holes in the 4" side for the people.

To shape the car shown in Figure IV-7, use a SurForm tool to taper the hood down toward the front. Then the entire front is smoothed into one sleek curve. The back is also turned into a continuous curve, although it's not tapered.

As with most toys, there are variations you can make and enjoy. If you start with a 12" piece of 2" x 4" board and drill eight holes for passengers plus one hole for a driver, you will have a streamlined bus.

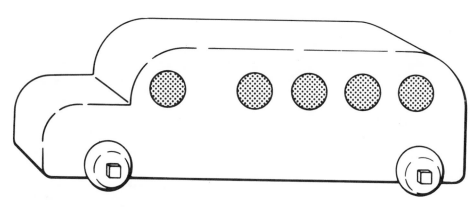

Figure IV-5. By "stretching out" the car with more wood and window holes, you obtain a bus

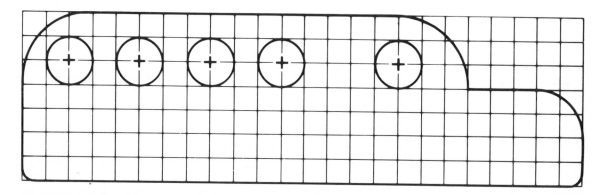

Figure IV-6. Using ½-inch squares, let whimsy—or your child— decide how long or short your pattern should be

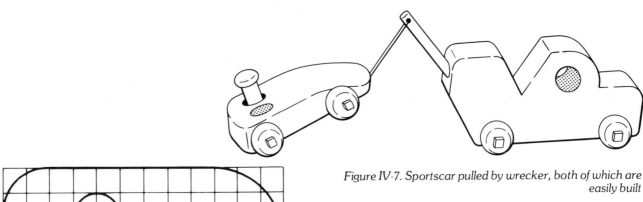

Figure IV-7. Sportscar pulled by wrecker, both of which are easily built

Figure IV-8. Lay out your sportscar on 1″ lumber using this pattern

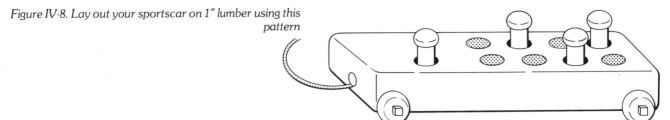

Figure IV-9. By "stretching" the sportscar shown above, you wind up with another kind of bus

AIRPLANE

The airplane's nose also requires extensive rounding off with a SurForm tool. The tailpiece can be left fairly straight, but don't forget to round off the sharp edges. This is a one-seater, so drill only one hole for the pilot. You can, however, add a second hole so a passenger can sit behind.

After you've completed all the shaping and sanding, simply glue the wing onto the body. Apply your wood sealer after the glue dries. You can fasten the wing with Elmer's Glue-All or any other common glue recommended for wood.

If Junior knocks off the wing in some rough play, just glue it back on. It can be a good real-life lesson in what happens when planes—even toy ones—get rough treatment. If you prefer to make sure the wing stays put, fasten two ¼″ by 1¼″ lag screws through the top of the wing and into the body.

WRECKER

The wrecker pictured in Figure IV-7 is built with saw, SurForm tool, drill, and sandpaper, just like the car and bus—until you're ready to make the boom that picks up disabled cars. There are a lot of toy wreckers in stores that have intricate mechanisms for booms and ropes that lift up and down—and even so, most of them don't lift up and down particularly well. Have you ever watched children play with such a wrecker? More often than not, after they get tired of trying to move the rope or boom, they grab a car and hoist it directly onto the elevated hook. So this design *begins* with an elevated hook. There aren't any moving parts on the wrecker (aside from wheels). That's up to every child's imagination—and that's what toys are supposed to encourage, right?

Use a ½″ or ¾″ dowel for the boom. A ¼″ dowel is too weak, and a 1″ dowel could split the 1½″ wrecker body.

Try to follow the slope of the wrecker's backside when you drill a hole about an inch deep to hold the boom dowel. Glue it into place. Figure IV-7 shows a 4″ long dowel (1″ is buried in the wrecker body).

The Catch

Now for the elevated hook to hold on to cars. Real wreckers and—unfortunately, from a safety point of view—some toy wreckers have real metal hooks. Ours has a simple, safe, but effective wood-and-string catch. (The same mechanism is used to couple the train.)

Fasten a piece of heavy string to the wrecker's boom dowel. An inch or so off the ground, fasten the string to a ¾″ long piece of ¼″ thick dowel. Then, using a ¼″ drill or bit, make a hole about ½″ deep near the very front of your sportscar bottom. With a saw, make a slanted groove from the back of the hole to about ¾″ up the front of your toy car. Figure IV-13 presents the idea graphically.

When the dowel is shoved into the hole, the string slips into the groove. There should be just enough pressure to keep the plug in the hole until Sis wants to tug it loose. You can tighten the fit by wrapping more string around the dowel, or loosen it by sanding the hole.

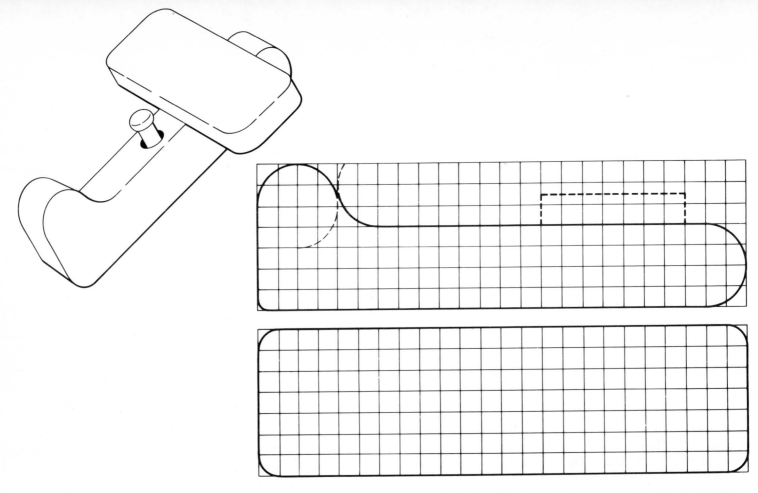

Figure IV-10-11. With a few pieces of wood, you or your children can assemble this airplane in a single evening. Lay your airplane body on 4″ x 2″ wood using this pattern and ½″ squares. The airplane's wing is executed from 1″ lumber, also using ½″ squares

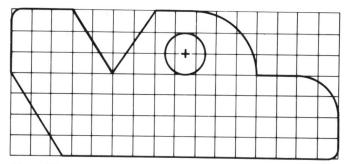

Figure IV-12. *The wrecker is rugged, safe, easy for little hands to maneuver—and simple for any size hands to build. Lay out your pattern on 2" wood, using ½" squares*

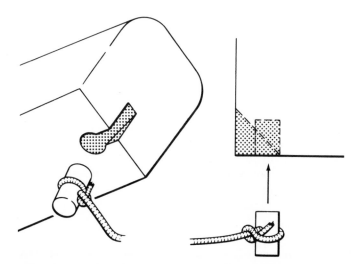

Figure IV-13. *The wrecker uses a catch made from string and wooden dowel, constructed as shown here*

If you make the hole and groove in the front of every truck, car, or bus you build, Junior can haul any of them away whenever the inspiration occurs. Don't forget to fit the airplane with this catch, too.

TRAIN

The train pictured here is just a beginning. You can add more cars, maybe with designs of your own.

The locomotive body is cut from a 2 x 4. The boiler section is a 5" length of closet pole. A dowel, either 1" or ½" thick, serves as the smokestack. A tall smokestack helps adults know it's a toy train. Your kids may never have seen one of the old coal burners with tall smokestacks, and the modern diesels have very short ones, so the one in Figure IV-14 is a compromise. The dowel is 1½" long. One inch *shows* and ½" is *glued into a hole* in the closet pole. Make it longer if you definitely want a coal burner, shorter for a diesel.

After you've glued the smokestack into place, use sandpaper or a SurForm tool to flatten the underside of the boiler section. Apply glue to the flat surface and to the end that will rest against the cab. A few rubber bands or some string will keep the surfaces tight while the glue dries.

The boxcar is simply an 8" piece of 2 x 4 with well-rounded corners. The coal car is sawed from a similar piece of wood. Use your imagination, hopefully whetted by now, to design other cars. For example, pieces of 2" x 4" board can become a caboose or a passenger car. A 1" x 4" or a 1" x 2" board can become a flatcar if you add a few dowels along the edges. Add more dowels plus a top, and

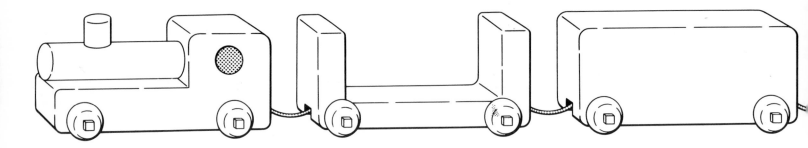

you have a circus car. A 1″ x 2″ base becomes a tank car when you glue on a length of closet pole.

The catch device for the wrecker and cars above is used on this train, too. The string's loose end is held by a short dowel. If your ¼″ hole and ¼″ dowel match rather well, you won't need any glue. The string alone should create a tight enough fit. I suggest this indirect fastening device so that in case the string breaks or wears out, you can pull out the dowel and quickly add a new string.

TRUCKS, TRUCKS, TRUCKS

Big trucks—tractors and trailers, as they're known in the trucking industry—are fantastic projects. They're so much fun, in fact, that I'm going to leave you a bit on your own. Our tractor (the front half of the big truck) is almost identical to the car and wrecker discussed above. Since you want the truck to look more rugged than a car, don't round off the corners into gentle curves. Simply sand or SurForm away the sharp edges for safety and durability.

I'm even going to let you sketch your own tractor onto the wood, with these hints: Look at the bus, car, and wrecker. Notice that the hood is 2″ high in all of them. It varies 1½″ to 2½″ long, so take your pick. The cab in the wrecker is about 2½″ long, including the curved and sloped portions. Since the cab of the truck doesn't slope very much, you might want to settle on a cab about 2″ long, but the choice is up to you.

There are a few variations for how long the back of the tractor should be. Two inches looks fine to me. That gives even a 4″ wide trailer enough room to swing out almost to 45 degrees. If you want your kids' trailers to be able to swing out even further, lengthen the backs out to 3″.

A ¼″ thick dowel should make a good peg for the back of your tractor. Mine would stick out about ½″, but make it longer or shorter if you want.

Working with children from about the age of 4 onward, you can design plenty of toys like this one. The *child* will show you how to abstract only the most basic aspects of the real-world machine into a toy. With this

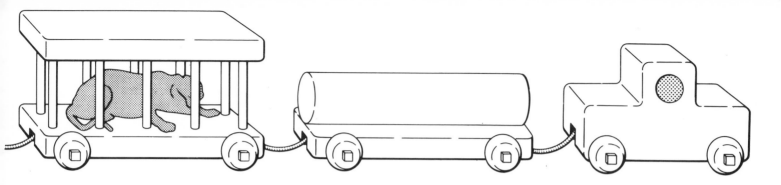

truck, for example, all you need are wheels, hood, cab, and window to make it look like a truck and perform like one. Adding too many details only limits what the imaginative child can visualize. Headlights, doors, door handles, bumpers, paint, and such may eventually fall off, but until they do, the child is stuck with them. Left simple and in natural wood, your truck can be red or blue, big or little, new or old, shiny or a wrecked heap. For science-oriented kids it's a space vehicle, or a tank for the military-minded.

Trailers for this truck project can be turned out literally by the dozens. I've picked three designs that turn me on (Figure IV-15). Evaluate them for yourself, and decide which you want to build or modify. They all clip onto the peg at the rear of the tractor.

The common semitrailer is simplest of all to make. It's just a piece of 2" x 4" board. I'd make it close to 12" long. Wheels come from spacers or closet poles, just as with the cars and buses.

You have to cut a piece 1" high and 2" long out of the front so the trailer can fasten onto the peg at the back of

Figure IV-14. With natural wood, rugged wheels, and catches between cars, a train like this can be built by parent-child or teacher-child teams over a fun-filled weekend. Lay out your locomotive onto 2" lumber using ½" penciled squares. The coal car also goes on 2" lumber, with ½" squares. Flatcars are simplicity itself, made from 1" lumber and short lengths of dowel. Passenger cars are little more than the open-air bus shown earlier, with sawed-off clothespin "people." The catch holding the cars together is effective, yet easy for small fingers to manipulate

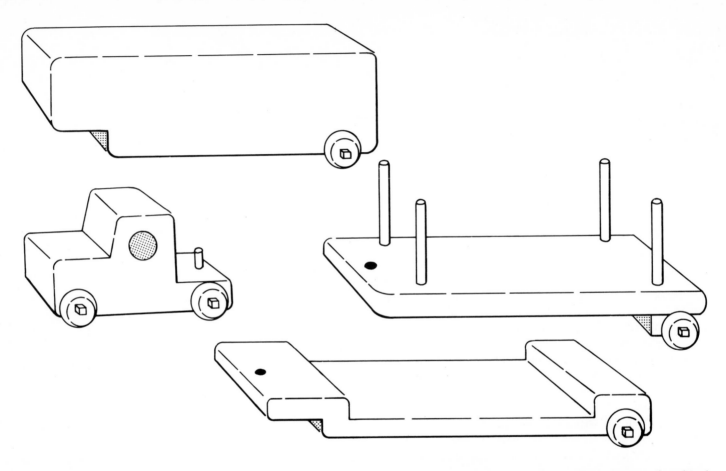

Figure IV-15. Trucks and trailers aplenty are yours for a bit of wood, some labor, and imagination. Shown here are only three of the dozens of trailers you—or your youngsters—can create

your tractor. Drill a ¼" hole (at least ½" deep) in your trailer that about matches the position of the peg. You may have to sandpaper the inside of the hole a bit so it can slip smoothly over the peg.

The flatbed trailer, second trailer from the top in Figure IV-15, can be built from a piece of 1" x 4" lumber as long as you want. I try to stick to 12". The wheels are mounted onto a small 1" piece of wood to raise the trailer enough so it will fit over the peg. (This assumes that you made the back platform on your tractor 1" thick.)

My sketch shows four dowels on the flatbed. That's generally enough to hold long logs and similar toys in place. If your children want more, drill more holes and slip in more ¼" pegs. I make mine 4" or so long, since longer dowels break too easily. Now that you're a fledgling toy designer, too, you can decide how long yours should be.

If you add even more pegs and cut out a top whose holes match the pegs in your bottom piece, you have a circus wagon. It probably won't matter to the kids whether the animals are kept securely inside. If you don't need pegs in front and back, the animals can slip in and out without doors. However, if the "insecure" cages bother you or your child, add a peg or two to the front and back. Drill the holes for one or two of the pegs all the way through the top board. Extend those pegs maybe ½" above the "ceiling" so they can be lifted up and down—and you've built a door in the cage. It makes a good coordination developer as well, since threading the peg through both holes is a demanding exercise for young hands. (This trailer is similar to the circus wagon in the train pictured earlier.)

The bottom trailer in Figure IV-15 looks just like the ones that carry heavy equipment to construction jobs. How long you make the bottom piece depends upon the length of your bulldozer, steam shovel, or similar toys. (They're going to be built in a later chapter.)

What other trailers can you design and build? Look at the trucks passing you in the street! Whatever you see—assuming you can see it as simply as your children do—you can build.

DRIVERS AND PASSENGERS

People can be fun to include in projects such as the airplane, passenger train, sportscar, bus, bulldozer. I wouldn't rush downtown for expensive tiny dolls or the brightly painted stylized figures sold with some of the expensive so-called educational toys. Instead, grab a handful of clothespins. Cut off the bottoms so you're left with only the top 2" or so. They make mighty fine people for the kids' toys. They aren't male or female, white or black, yellow or red, young or old, rich or poor—they're just people.

5 *Toys that work*

(3 to 12 years to play with; 10 years and up to build, with some guidance needed for some youngsters.) Skills: Not difficult, but a bit of patience helps.

When little boys and girls get to be maybe 3 years old, they start looking for toys that have moving parts. The moving parts help them to test their coordination and figure out the spatial relationships in their world, but won't interfere with fertile imaginations as long as the toy designer leaves something for the imagination to do.

Figure V-1. This bulldozer is one of the best sandbox or playroom toys, made from a few pieces of wood and hardware

BULLDOZER

The bulldozer pictured here, complicated-looking though it may be, can be built in an evening.

Materials:

8″ piece of 2″ x 4″ hardwood or pine.

8″ piece of 1″ x 4″ hardwood or pine.

Two pieces of 9″ long dowels, 1″ in diameter.

Eight wheels (spacers or closet pole slices).

1″ length of ¼″ dowel.

Eight pieces of ¼″ x 1½″ lag screws.

Two pieces of ¼″ x 2″ lag screws.

Round off the edges and corners of the two boards and one end of the dowels. Drill a ½″ hole for the driver and a ¼″ hole for the "engine" exhaust pipe in the bulldozer body. Then fasten the wheels into place, four on each side almost

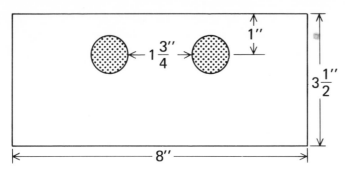

Figure V-2. How to form and drill the "plow"

touching each other. (See Chapter 4 for advice on making and installing the wheels.)

Figure V-2 shows how to lay out the 1″ holes you drill in the pusher board. Stop short of drilling entirely through the 1″ board so your work will end up strong. Before you glue the dowels into the pusher, however, drill a ¼″ hole in each dowel about an inch from its rounded end.

Assuming that your dowels fit snugly into the pusher holes, glue alone should hold them together. If the bulldozer will be a beach toy, waterproof glue is recommended, but it's not critical.

You can strengthen the pusher assembly by carefully driving a nail through the top, down through the dowel, and back into the pusher board. That requires a 1″ or longer finishing nail. Even if you use nails, glue the pieces together, too.

After the pusher assembly is ready, position it as close as possible to the bulldozer's body. Ideally it will rest against the front of the toy. Before you fasten the dowels to your bulldozer's body, be sure that the lag screws slip easily through the hole in each dowel. You don't want the threads to hold on to the dowel, only the body. When Sis gets the urge, she'll want to raise the pusher.

Push a 2″ long lag screw through the hole in your dowel and twist it into the body. Stop just short of tightening the screw completely; you want a bit of space left so the dowel can pivot up and down with the pusher.

Glue your exhaust pipe into its hole. Finish the bulldozer according to the wisdom expressed in Chapter 4. Slip a sawed-off clothespin into the driver's seat, and start up the engine!

DIGGING STEAM SHOVEL

Steam shovel toys have always bugged me. Some look just great, and lots of them have levers and chains, cords or wires that are supposed to make them move up, down, sideways, fill up, and dump. A few of those elaborate, expensive toys actually do operate to a degree—for a while, anyway. But almost none of them can pick up sand from a beach! What good is a steam shovel if it can't pick up sand?

Here's a design that works even on the beach. And it's going to keep on working because there is only one moving part, which you're going to couple directly to one of the most efficient machines ever invented—*your child's hand.*

You can build this simple-but-sure steam shovel in an evening or two. Chapter 4 tells how to select the wood, build and install the wheels, and finish the project.

Materials:

Base:

2″ x 4″ board, 8″ long [A].

Body:

bottom, 2″ x 4″ board, 8″ long [B].
sides, two pieces, 1″ x 4″ board 8″ long [C].
top, 2″ x 4″ board, *about* 5″ long [D].

Boom:

2″ x 4″ board, 12″ long [E].

Digger:

pole, ¾″ dowel, 16″ long [F].
left side, 1″ x 4″ board, 4″ long [G].
right side, 1″ x 4″ board, 3¼″ long [H].

bottom, 1″ x 4″ board, 3¼″ long (rounded and tapered) [J].

Ten wheels (spindle spacers or ¾″ slices of closet pole).

Hardware:

Sixteen pieces, 3″ finishing nails.
Fourteen pieces, 1½″ finishing nails.
Ten pieces, ¼″ x 1½″ lag screws.
One piece, ¼″ x 3″ lag screws.
Two pieces, ¼″ washers.

To assemble this toy, first drill a ¼″ hole completely through the base [A] at its very center. Sand it until the longest lag screw slips easily through the hole. If you own an electric drill, make in the bottom of the body [B] an ⅛″ pilot hole that exactly matches the ¼″ hole. (Without a drill, drive in a nail and then pull it out.) This pilot hole protects against your splitting the bottom board when you turn the lag screw deep into the wood, and also guarantees greater accuracy in lining up the base and the cab—even though such accuracy really isn't critical. But don't fasten the base and body bottom together just yet.

Fasten the two 1″ x 4″ sidepieces [C] onto the 2″ x 4″ bottom [B]. Use glue, plus three or four 3″ finishing nails.

If you want to conceal the nails here and elsewhere, punch the nail head about ⅛″ into the wood with a *nail set* or another nail. Plug the resulting hole with plastic wood and when it's dry, sand it smooth. Or drill ³⁄₁₆″ pilot holes and use ¼″ lag screws, letting them show for a more rugged appearance.

The boom is cut from 2″ x 4″ lumber. Figure V-4

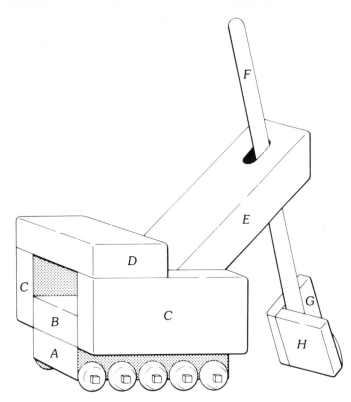

Figure V-3. The steam shovel shown here came about as a result of my frustration at never being able to find one in stores that met my expectations

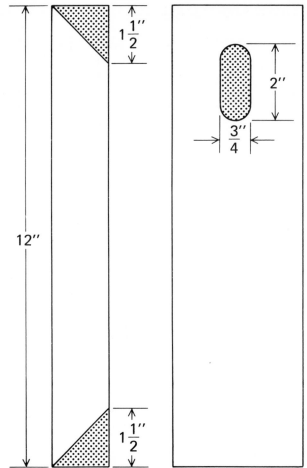

Figure V-4. Steam shovel "boom" (E) is cut from piece of 2" x 4" lumber according to this sketch

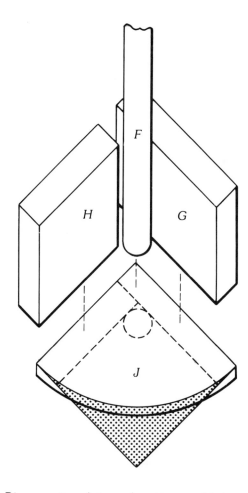

Figure V-5. Digger portion of steam shovel is assembled as shown

shows how to make the 45-degree-angled cuts at top and bottom. If your square has a 45-degree setting as well as 90 degrees, that's the easiest way to mark the cut. If not, then use a ruler. Figure V-4 shows how to measure the slope instead of drawing it to 45 degrees with a "square," assuming that your "2 x 4" is actually only 1½" wide. So if you measure 1½" from the edge, you'll have a 45-degree cut too. If your particular boards are wider or narrower, adjust that dimension accordingly.

The groove for the digger dowel [F] is simple to make. First mark the ¾" wide by 2" long groove. Then bore a ¾" hole exactly at each end. Use a sabre saw or coping saw to join the holes, and there's your slot. Roll up some sandpaper to smooth it out. In case you don't own a ¾" bit, you can accomplish the whole trick with a 1" bit. In that case, use a 1" dowel instead of a ¾" one. This design ensures that the digger will move easily from front to back, but won't move sideways very much. That's how real steam shovels work.

Set your boom [E] into the body to make sure everything fits OK. The bottom edge of the boom should touch the inside corners of the sidepieces. Before you glue and nail it permanently into place, draw 45-degree lines on the outsides of both sides. The lines should parallel the bottom of the boom and help you get your nails in the right place.

Apply glue generously to the sides and angled bottom of the boom. Then slip it into place. Drive three or four nails from the sides into the boom. And, finally, drive another two or three nails from the boom into the bottom board.

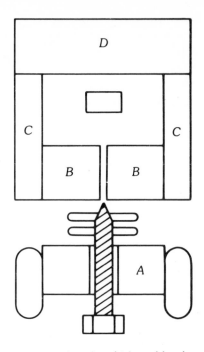

Figure V-6. The pivot on your steam shovel—which enables the "cab" to rotate—shown in cross section

Now you can build the digger. Carefully glue and nail the larger 1″ x 4″ board [G] onto the smaller one [H]. Use 1½″ finishing nails and proceed according to Figure V-5.

The bottom piece [J], also cut from 1″ x 4″ wood, has to be rounded. You can saw the curve (using a 3¼″ radius) or carve it with your SurForm tool. The entire curved area has to be tapered with SurForm tool or sandpaper—preferably both. Don't whittle it down quite to a point, because the point will only chip away as the digger encounters stones and other hard objects. But you do have to taper it substantially so it slips smoothly into the beach or sandpile.

The shaped bottom piece is glued and nailed to the inside of the already-assembled pieces. Flatten the bottom 3¾″ of the dowel so the flat areas match the rest of your digger's claw. If you lay the gadget at the corner of a table, you can hold the dowel in place while you drive nails. Don't forget to hammer at least one nail from the bottom into the dowel.

Finish and seal the wood before you fasten the body to the base via its lag-screw pivot. Figure V-6 offers an exploded view of how to assemble the steam shovel body to its base via a pivot. Don't tighten the lag screw all the way. You need a tiny gap so the top can pivot smoothly around the base.

There's just a chance that the head of your lag screw may extend below the bottom of your wheels. Closet poles and spindle spacers come in a variety of sizes, so it's hard to plan ahead for all of them. In case that happens, take out the lag screw and bore a shallow ¾″ or 1″ hole with your brace and bit that will recess the lag-screw head in the bottom of the base and keep it out of the way.

Slip the digger into the boom's slot, and the steam shovel is ready for its test dig. I'd advise you to turn the steam shovel over to the kids right away. If you play with it, you're probably going to want one of your own—but building the second one will be even easier than building the first.

The entire toy operates from one lever—the extended dowel on the digger. You push the digger down into the sand and force it forward to pick up a full scoop. Still holding the "joy stick," you pivot the steam shovel body over to the dump truck you'll build next. Twist your wrist and the digger rolls over, dumping its load neatly into the truck. Pivot back again, and repeat. If you have to move the steam shovel to a new location, just shove it there. Its ten wheels, which have the actual appearance of tracks used on real steam shovels, keep the toy from getting mired in loose sand.

DUMP TRUCK

A dump truck that really dumps is a nice companion to the bulldozer and steam shovel. If you built the tractor-truck unit in the last chapter, you already have *half* a dump truck. Now you just have to design a sand-dumping back that hooks onto the tractor's peg.

With three 12″ long pieces of 1″ x 4″ pine or hardwood, you can put together the rough shape of the dumping back. Box off the front by nailing and gluing in

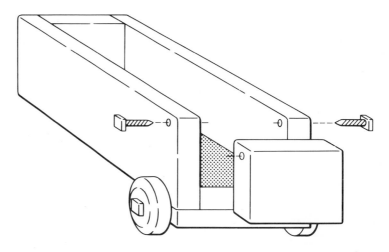

Figure V-7. Dump-truck back for the truck body shown earlier makes a logical and enjoyable addition to any playroom or sandbox

another piece of 1 x 4 as long as your "4 inch" board is wide (about 3½"). The back is boxed off with a board of the same size—but don't glue or nail it permanently into place. Round off the bottom of the back piece—"the gate," in truckers' parlance—so it swings easily. And drill ¼" holes in the edges according to Figure V-7. The holes receive the ends of two 1" long ¼" lag screws. The screws form pivots in the holes.

When Junior fills his dump truck with sand, it stays put until he reaches the construction site. Then, when he slips the back loose from the truck's peg and dumps it, the sand pushes against the gate, forces it open, and spills freely from the dump truck.

If you were to pivot the gate near the bottom instead of the top, you wouldn't have a dump truck but a common *gate-back truck*. And that's just about how easy it is to design your own toys.

6 Toys *that float*

Boats can be fun whether on a whitecapped pond in the park, in the soapy bathtub, or simply shoved across a tiled playroom floor. When I was a boy, toy boats were often magnificent creations that sailed like real ones, looked like real ones, were built like real ones. But back then, young children didn't often get them because they were fragile and expensive. Today's boys and girls seldom get these boats because they aren't available in most toy stores. It's a shame, too, because we have glues and materials to make them stronger, and manufacturing methods to make them cheaper than ever before.

"STEAMBOATS"

(18 months to 8 years to play with; 6 to 10 years to build.)
Skills: Very easy.
Materials: Scrap of lumber. Two short pieces of dowel.

"Steamboats" can be as simple or as elaborate as you or your children want to make them. Figure VI-2 shows one that's about as simple as they come. You can cut the bottom, rakishly pointed in front, from almost any scrap of lumber you find. Round off the point a bit, of course. The smokestacks are dowels slipped into holes you bore *almost through* the hull. Glue the dowels into place *after* you sandpaper the project. If the boat won't ever float in

real water, you can leave the wood in its natural state.

For real water, you'll need real finish. Polyurethane wood sealers described in Chapter 3 do a fine job of water-proofing. If you want color, many of the child-safe paints work fine. If the boat's going to really get soaked, use paint first, followed by polyurethane sealer.

If you're really going to get into boat making and sailing, check out *spar varnish.* If you read the labels, you'll see that almost all spar varnish is child-safe. It protects boats without hiding the colors, and lends a brilliant gloss to the finish.

CABIN CRUISER

(18 months to 10 years to play with; 6 to 10 years to build.)
Skills: Very easy.
Materials: Two scraps of lumber. Three pieces of dowel.

The next drawing shows how to embellish the basic boat a bit. Start out with the same sort of hull, an odd-shaped piece of wood cut to a point in front (then rounded a bit). This time, add a "cabin" to the boat plus a flagpole. Even though it won't be in proportion to the rest of the boat, I wouldn't use a dowel thinner than ¼" for the flagpole or it'll break too easily. You can buy flags ready-made in dime,

Figure VI-1. Whether on a lake or the kitchen table, this "birthday cake boat" is eye-catching—yet assembled from odd-sized bits of wood

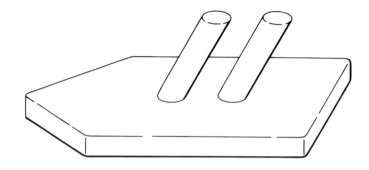

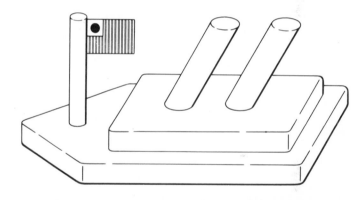

Figure VI-2. One-tiered steamboat (above) with either one or two smokestacks, can be assembled in half an hour from scraps of lumber. Below is a version for fancier tastes or more detailed imaginations

art, novelty, or stationery stores, but they're easy to make for yourself.

Glue is generally strong enough to hold a boat like this together, but since parents over 30 seldom trust glue, you can also add a few finishing nails. If you drive them in from underneath, nobody will ever see them.

YACHT

(18 months to 10 years to play with; 6 to 10 years to build.)
Skills: Easy.
Materials: Three or four scraps of lumber. Three pieces of dowel. Couple of dozen upholstery tacks (optional).

To create a really impressive-looking boat, carry the details and layers of wood as far as you want. One way of adding "windows" is to simply bore ¼" or ½" holes a short way into the wood with a drill or a brace and bit. In Photo VI-1, however, the windows are upholstery tacks driven in all around the deck levels.

To keep this design from capsizing in the water, you probably have to add extra weight to the bottom. Duplicate the middle-sized board, and fasten it underneath your boat. If you build a boat much taller than this, you'll probably have to counterbalance it even further on the bottom.

There's one sure way to find out how stable a boat is in the water: try it! If it topples over or doesn't sit upright,

add more weight to the bottom. If it floats just right, dry off your project, finish it, and launch it.

MOTOR BOATS

(4 to 12 years to play with; 10 years and up to build without supervision.)
Skills: Easy, but some careful sawing and fitting required.
Materials: Sundry scraps of lumber and/or Masonite.

You can add motors to boats like these. No, you don't have to invest in gasoline or battery-driven power sources. Just grab a handful of rubber bands.

Figure VI-3 shows a paddle wheel on the back of one of our simpler boats. You can adapt almost any boat to hold a similar gadget. Figure VI-4 shows how to cut the parts for the paddle wheel and Figure VI-5 shows how to assemble the two pieces.

You can choose from several types of material for the paddle wheel, depending upon what scraps you have on hand or can pick up cheaply at a lumberyard, hardware, or art store. Plexiglas plastic, ¹⁄₁₆" to ⅛" thick, is ideal if you know how to work with it. Masonite, ⅛" to ¼" thick, works well, too. You can use ¼" plywood or even cut the paddle-wheel parts from very stiff cardboard, but you'll have to waterproof either material very well with varnish or paint.

To make the paddle wheels fit boats of different sizes, draw the squares in Figure VI-4 to match the proportions of the hull. For a paddle wheel that fits on the back of a 6"

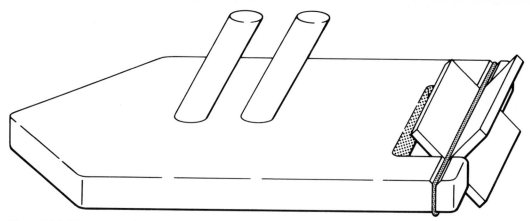

Figure VI-3. It's not exactly the African Queen, *but its paddle wheel does work*

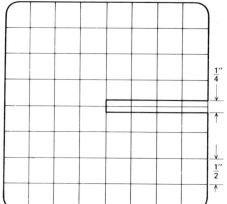

Figure VI-4.

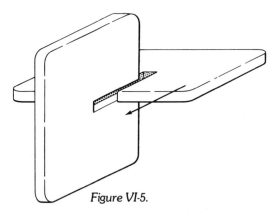

Figure VI-5.

The paddle wheel pattern. The exact size varies to match the boat you've built: for a 4″ paddle wheel suitable for a boat about 6″ wide, use ½″ squares to copy this pattern. On smaller boats use ¼″ or ⅜″ squares, or larger squares for larger models. The

slot's width should equal the thickness of the paddle itself. In other words, if your paddle is cut from ¼″ plywood, make a ¼″ slot. Assemble the paddle wheel's components as shown, then glue them securely

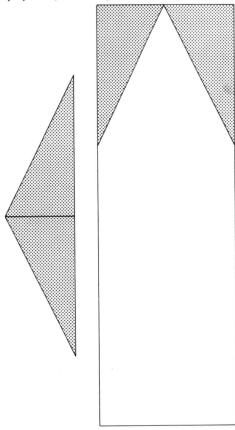

Figure VI-6. Simple sailboat made from 1" thick scrap lumber, wooden dowel, scrap of cloth, and string or rope

Figure VI-7. After making two cuts to form the pointed bow, glue and/or nail the two resulting triangles (shaded) to the bottom to form a keel

wide boat, draw your lines about ½" apart. For bigger boats, try ¾" lines. For smaller ones, use ¼" or ⅜" lines.

After you glue the paddle wheel parts together, slip several rubber bands around it and fasten the loose ends to the two grooves sawed or filed in the end of your boat. Wind up the rubber band motor (backwards), set it in the water, and let it go.

SAILBOAT

(5 and up to play with; 10 and up to build.)
Skills: Easy.
Materials: A 1" board. Dowel. Heavy string or light rope. Small piece of cloth.

Sailboats are the epitome of romance, adventure, natural motive power, beauty. They can be as easy or as hard to build as you wish.

Photo VI-6 shows one of the simplest sailboats imaginable. It isn't much more than our simplest steamboat fitted with a sail instead of smokestacks. Pick dimensions that fit the materials you have at hand or can buy cheaply.

For stability, a sailboat needs a *keel,* a flat projection beneath the boat that keeps it from tipping over in the wind. In this simple sailboat, build a primitive keel from the two parts cut off to form the pointed front. Figure VI-7 shows graphically what I'm talking about. Since you can make this sailboat out of any size wood, simply measure the width of your board and use that same measurement to figure out where your boat's point should end. Then glue and nail the pieces to the bottom of your hull, patch up any gaps in the keel with plastic wood and, when it dries, smooth off the whole structure.

On real boats, the keels' outer edges are generally steamlined almost to points. Since you don't plan to set any speed records with this simple craft, you can leave the keel unstreamlined.

Don't use anything thinner than a ½" dowel for the mast unless you're sure that your youngsters can cope with the challenge and potential splinters of thinner masts.

Almost any kind of fabric can be used for sails. If the cloth is too heavy, it'll slow down the ship. Nylon and other synthetics hold up when wet. Cotton duck and similar light but hearty fabrics are OK, too. An old sheet works just dandy.

Stitch wide enough hems along the two appropriate edges so that the mast can slip into one hem and the boom —the piece that keeps the bottom of the sail rigid—into the other. A ¼" dowel is ideal for the boom. In your hemming, close off the top so the mast won't slip through, and close off both ends of the boom—after inserting it, of course.

To keep the sail in place as it bellows out from the wind, tie a short piece of cord or rope between a screw eye at the end of the boom and a screw eye at the very back of the hull. For finishing touches, I ran a rope through screw eyes placed strategically all around the deck.

*Figure VI-8. A catamaran that you can build alone—
or with your kids' help*

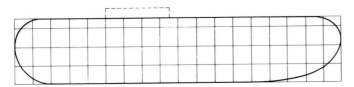

*Figure VI-9. Lay the hulls for the catamaran out on 2" x 4"
lumber, using ½" squares. The appropriate size of the
catamaran's traverse body is shown in broken line*

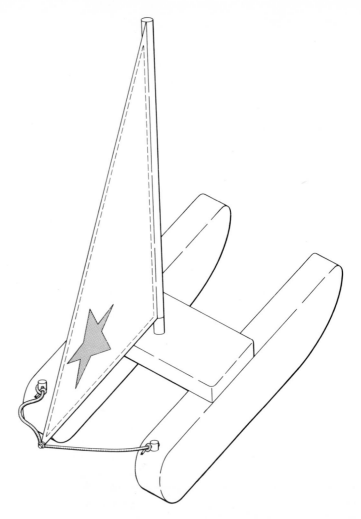

62

CATAMARAN

(5 and up to play with; 10 and up to build.)
Skills: Easy.
Materials: 2" x 4" pine, 32" long.
1" x 4" pine, 8" long.
½" dowel, 18" long (mast).
¼" dowel, 11" long (boom).
Small piece of cloth (sail).

For stability, almost nothing beats the catamaran. My version, which can be yours, too, is shown in Figure VI-8. The two hulls are cut from pieces of 2 x 4, each 16" long. The body you fasten atop the double hulls is an 8" long piece of 1 x 4. With 18" mast, the pictured catamaran has plenty of cloth to capture the wind and sail like a demon. If you're more interested in a landlubber's toy than a real sailing ship, you might want to shorten the mast. Conversely, you can make the mast higher, the boom longer, and even add a second sail forward of the mast.

Cut your chosen fabric into a right-angle triangle at least 10" wide and 17" high. You should hem it all the way around to keep the fabric from fraying. If you choose to do it that way, you can make the hem wide enough on the two appropriate sides that you can slip in the boom and the mast described in the earlier sailboat project.

The most nautical way to attach your sail is with heavy thread. Fasten it onto the boom first, then the mast. Alternatively, you can use thread only at the very ends of the boom and mast. Midway you can use small curtain rings to keep the sail close to the mast, it doesn't have to fit snugly against the dowel.

Two pegs sunk into the rear of each catamaran hull hold the "ropes" that in turn hold the sail in place as it gathers wind. To make the most of a good wind, the sail should blow out to an angle of maybe 30 degrees. These ropes let the sail twist to that angle, but no further. You need to allow the boom to turn the sail either right or left, depending on how the wind is blowing. That's why there are two ropes at the end of the boom. The other end of the boom fits into a small hole that you drill into the mast, being sure that it remains free to pivot.

Don't fasten the body permanently onto your catamaran until it's had a couple of test sailings. Depending on the type of wood used, how you shape the hulls, and how heavy your sails are, the body may have to go afore or astern of where I show it in Figure VI-8. Four finishing nails can hold the boat together temporarily while you conduct your sea tests.

SUPER-SAILER

(8 and up to play with; 12 and up to build.)
Skills: Kind of demanding; not a good first project.
Materials: 2" x 4" pine, 12" long.
¼" plywood, 8" x 4".
½" dowel, 16" long.
Cloth for sails.

For one of the best sailing and finest-looking boats around, try your hand at the one pictured in Figure VI-10, cut from a 12" long piece of 2" x 4" pine. If you were to hand-carve this hull, you'd be at it until the sea dried up, so I've drawn a way to make the initial cuts with a common handsaw.

Sketch the top markings from Figure VI-11 onto your 2" x 4" and saw away. Then sketch the side markings and make those saw cuts. Figure VI-12 shows how the various patterns progressively shape the hull.

Attack the hull with a SurForm tool to round off all the corners. Pay special attention to getting a shape up front that pleases you or your children. Then drill ½" holes for the mast and, assuming you want them to go along for a ride, the clothespin people.

Flip over the hull and get ready to add a keel. Any of the materials recommended for the paddle wheel earlier in this chapter will work for your keel. Best of all, I feel, is ¼" plywood. Cut the keel according to Figure VI-13. Then use a SurForm tool and sandpaper to feather down the edges until they're thin and streamlined. Leave the flat top of the keel alone; you want that to fit tightly into a groove we'll saw into the bottom of the hull.

Assuming you used ¼" plywood, measure a ¼" wide groove along the very center of your hull. Place your handsaw *well inside* one of the lines and saw about ¼" to ⅜" deep. Do the same inside the other line. The easiest way to remove the wood from between the two lines is with a small wood chisel. Lacking that, you can improvise with an old screwdriver. You can also keep sawing at various spots within the groove marks until all of the *excess* wood is sawed away. (If you build a keel that's other than ¼" thick, you'll have to draw a groove of appropriate dimensions, of course.)

Figure VI-10. Super-Sailer, one of the finest toy sailboats ever to make the do-it-yourself scene, is not beyond the abilities of novice toymakers —nor their kids

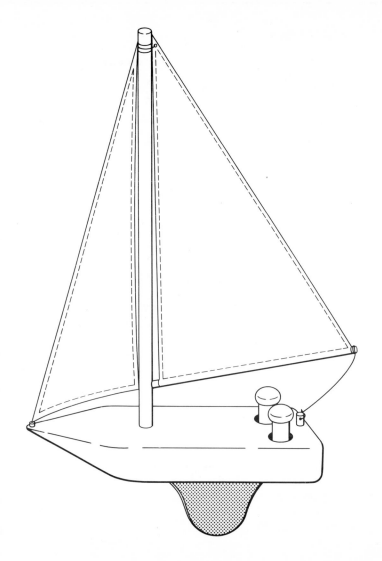

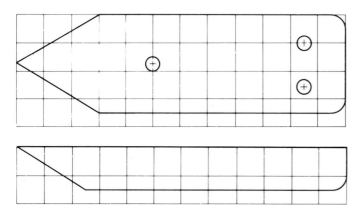

Figure VI-11. To prepare the hull's top (above), lay out a grid of 1″ squares or simply make measurements. Below: how your hull's profile should look, according to the same scale

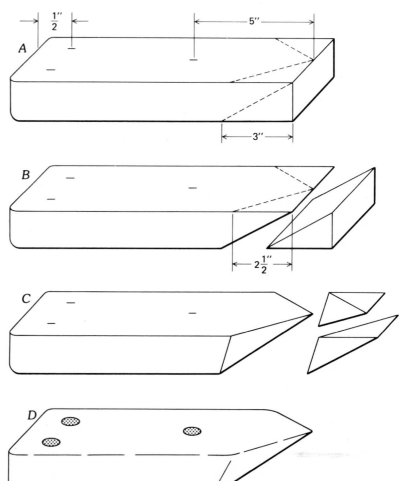

Figure VI-12. A shows how your block of 2″ x 4″ wood will look just before you start sawing. Cuts for horizontal lines will leave the hull looking like B. Vertical cuts in the piece should leave it looking like C. After both the horizontal and vertical saw cuts are made, shape the hull into a smooth curve (D) with SurForm tool or other implements

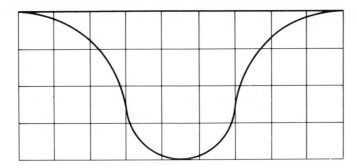

Figure VI-13. The keel, which holds the boat steady in the water even under strong winds, is cut from ¼″ plywood or the like. Lay out this pattern using 1″ squares, or draw the bottom curve with a compass set to a 1½″ radius. Setting the compass for a 3″ radius will form the larger side curves

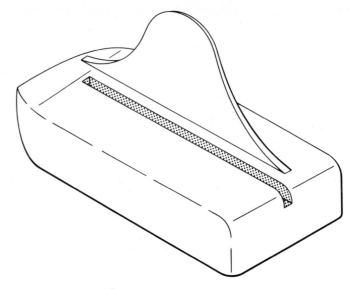

Figure VI-14. Affix the keel to the hull like this

Proceed carefully. Be sure that the groove is considerably too tight at first. Try to slip the keel into the groove, and then sandpaper the groove until you're just barely able to force the keel in. Then glue it there. You may have to use a bit of plastic wood to fill up irregularities where the keel meets the hull.

Now you're ready to finish the sailboat. Natural wood protected with spar varnish or wood sealer looks nice. Or you might want to stain the wood before sealing it. Maple, walnut, and mahogany impart a rich, woodsy look to pine boards.

If you decide to use paint, pick out something very glossy and bright. Model airplane dope is about the shiniest, brightest stuff available; it dries fast, too. You can apply half a dozen coats of dope in a single day. Sandpaper lightly (using superfine grade sandpaper) between coats (or at least after every other coat) to remove bubbles, bristles, and slight irregularities. When you're finished, your sailboat will outshine even the most expensive toy-store models.

To rig this sailboat, cut two sails. When hemmed, one should be about 14″ high and 8″ wide at the bottom, the other should be 14″ high and 5″ wide at the bottom.

Fasten the big sail to its boom with thread, or with tiny curtain rings along it plus thread at its two ends. Secure it to the mast in the same fashion. The smaller sail (the *spinnaker,* in nautical jargon) is fastened only with "ropes" made of thread or cord. First, secure it to the mast. Then, allowing 1″ or 2″ of extra line, fasten the other end to a small peg near the very front of the boat. That arrangement isn't going to make the bottom of the sail too taut, but it's not supposed to. The spinnaker should be loose enough to billow out in a good wind.

The boom on the larger sail should be secured to another peg with a length of "rope" about a foot long. You'll usually have only 6″ or so of the line played out when you sail this mighty vessel. But it looks shipshape to have the extra line coiled around the "windlass," and it gives you sailing versatility.

7 A building for all reasons

(3 to 10 years to play with; 6 and up to build simple furnishings. 10 and up for the rest.)
Skills: Very easy.
Materials: ½ sheet of ¼" plywood or several cardboard boxes. Household doodads.

This project shows what a bit of imagination can do with a well-designed toy. Unlike more conventional dollhouses, this one doesn't have exterior walls that prevent young hands from reaching all parts of the building. So, in this design, the roof, inside walls, floor, and fertile imaginations make the four outside walls *seem* real. But there's open

Figure VII-1. Dollhouse—or any other kind of house or building— made from easily-obtained materials

space for tiny hands (or large ones) to reach every inch of playing area.

However, with this single construction project, you're going to make more than a dollhouse. Without changing the building at all, it's going to be 1) a dollhouse; 2) a barn with room for horses and cows; 3) a garage capable of fixing broken toy cars; 4) a hospital; 5) a school; 6) anything else young minds want to place within "four walls."

I can see only one reason why manufacturers turn out one building they call a house, another they call a barn, and then yet another labeled "garage"—that way, they can sell you three buildings instead of one. On top of that, all too many parents are suckers for the painted rugs, painted walls, shingles and shutters, and dozens of fragile pieces of

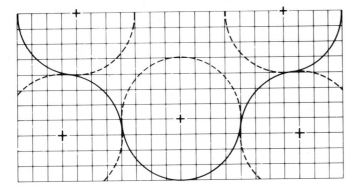

Figure VII-2. Shape the roof pieces from this pattern. You can draw the grid of 1" squares onto your cardboard or plywood— but it's far easier to use a compass, set to a 4" radius, to draw the arcs that will form the neatly-curved roof. This pattern is for half the roof, so you'll need to make two exact (or almost exact) copies

furniture and other doodads crammed into such commercially made buildings.

The house pictured here was made out of cheaper corrugated cardboard. But there's so much support for the walls and roof that the cardboard is strong enough for most hard-playing youngsters. You can really do it up proud, however, by using ¼" plywood.

Complex as the roof may seem, it's a dream to draw. Simply set your compass (or makeshift string and nail compass) to draw circles with 4" radii. Set the point down wherever "X" marks the five spots in Figure VII-2, and the curvaceous lines literally fall into pattern for one half of the roof.

If you're using cardboard, make the roof from a single piece that's 22" square. Trace the pattern from Figure VII-2 onto the square twice. If you work with plywood, make two separate pieces. Use sandpaper or the SurForm tool to shave away a bit of the lower edges of the wooden roof pieces where they will meet when you assemble the building later.

The walls feature curved archways for a couple of reasons. One, they look nice. Two, they're shaped like the hands that will want to shove people, animals, and cars through them. And three, the curved tops are much stronger than squared ones. (If you ran a straight cut across the top of each doorway, that line would match the slots cut for fitting the two wall pieces together. The resulting lineup would produce what engineers call a "stress point," where the walls would bend relatively easily.)

70

If you're working with plywood, you can cut out the archways with a coping saw or electric sabre saw. With cardboard, use a small knife or single-edged razor blade. First make a very light cut so you can carefully follow the pencil line. Then make several passes over the line with your blade, slicing more deeply with each pass. After you've cut deeply enough, you'll be left with a smooth, professional-looking archway.

Surprisingly enough, cardboard takes on a sharp edge when you cut it. I always "smooth" off the edges with sandpaper. With plywood, round off all the edges with a SurForm tool and/or sandpaper. Do these finishing touches before assembling the house.

The slots in the walls allow the two wall pieces to slip together neatly. For ¼″ plywood, you'll need about a ¼″ slot. For cardboard, the slot has to be closer to ⅛″. Make the slots too small at first, then slowly expand them until you get a neat, tight fit. Notice that the slot in the wall which is straight across the top is not exactly in the middle. This gives us rooms of different sizes.

Here's the rationale for the base's design. Since to err is human, it would be tough to line up all the base and wall pieces precisely. To do so, you'd have to engage in a lot of sanding. Instead, let's deliberately build a terrace look to the outside edges of this toy building. The bottom piece is 21½″ square. The walls are 21″ long, which allows a ¼″ margin all the way around. The base supports are an additional ¼″ smaller than the walls. When the entire project is assembled, the terrace lends a neat, finished look

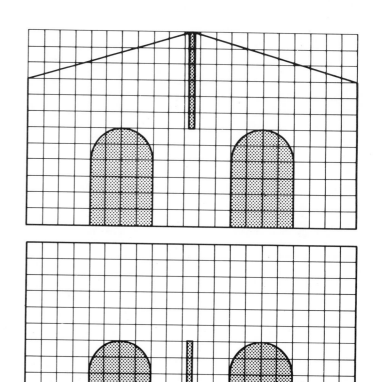

Figure VII-3. Patterns for each of the two walls, measured on a grid of 1″ squares. The vertical slots should be as wide as the plywood or cardboard you're working with

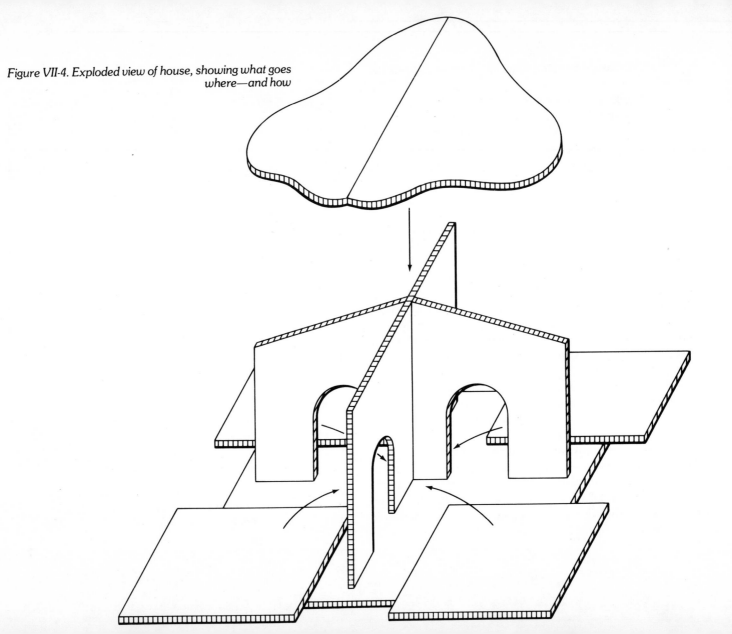

Figure VII-4. Exploded view of house, showing what goes where—and how

to the whole thing. And it's strong! Keep this trick in mind when you design your own toys.

Here are the dimensions for the base pieces you have to cut:

Bottom:

21½″ x 21½″ (1 piece)

Terrace:

11½″ x 10¼″ (2 pieces)

8¾″ x 10¼″ (2 pieces)

Assemble the building this way:

1. Slip the two wall pieces together and set them on top of the large base piece. Make sure there's an even space all the way around, about ¼″.

2. Fit two or three of the base terrace pieces into place just to be sure that the walls are aligned squarely.

3. Mark where the walls will be located on the bottom piece and spread a generous bead of glue along that line. (The various white glues such as Elmer's Glue-All are strong enough, and any excess becomes transparent when dry.)

4. Set the walls into their final resting place.

5. Apply a generous layer of glue to the bottom of one base terrace piece and set it into place. Do likewise for the other three terrace pieces.

6. Make sure that the roof fits on top of the walls. Then spread a generous bead of glue along the upper edge of the walls and quickly press the roof into place. (With plywood, be sure to glue the two roof pieces to each other as well.)

Once the glue has dried (give it an hour or so), your finished building will be ready for its first occupant. With

Figure VII-5. Basic furniture and people, assembled from corks, scrap wood, clothespins, etc.

cardboard, I prefer to leave the edges exposed. The corrugated inner piece makes a rugged-looking detail looking very much like the ironwork inside big buildings downtown. On plywood, I'd be inclined to use wood sealer that leaves the building with a natural-wood appearance.

How to Play With the Building

There's nothing patently wrong with dollhouses, assuming they're used well. But I don't like to see only girls given dollhouses, while only boys are given garages. Nobody's yet been able to demonstrate that if parents choose rugged he-man toys for boys, they'll become rugged he-men; or if parents pick only dolls and dishes for girls, they'll become delicate, demure young women. But plenty of researchers have found strong evidence that parents can confuse kids by strongly pushing selected interests at them.

The social scientists I stay in touch with feel that toys may help children form a sharper picture of the real world. Think of them as a stage with props on which our boys and girls act out the roles that parents, teachers, or other adults sketch for them. If you take this very generalized building to a child and say, "Here's a dollhouse," you may be insinuating that choice is limited to household sur-roundings. On the other hand, if you say, "Here's a building. Either you alone or both of us together can make it into a house, school, garage, or barn," probably you're broadening the way the child looks at the options open to him. From the studies I've seen, we probably can't make much impact on what options our children eventually do choose. You can, however, expose them to as many options as you can find.

My friend Flo Kerckhoff at Purdue University's Child Development Laboratories tells me that many parents fool themselves into believing that children will absorb from them by example. "Children do not absorb much," she says. "They must be taught most of what they learn, and today they have a great deal of teaching from a tremendous number of influences outside the home. If parents want to have influence, they will have to first make time for their parenthood, and then speak loudly and clearly and often to be heard."

That's what I'm trying to help you with.

First of all, build this House for All Reasons *with* your children. If you have very young children, you can build it *for* them, but make sure they're on hand to hand you tools, glue, pieces of the house. Once it's built, let the kids decide the decoration. The decoration can change from day to day—it would take at least a hundred coats of paint and wallpaper before the walls would start collapsing from the weight. But don't be shocked if Junior and Sis decide to let the plain brown walls stay the way they are—in their minds, the walls, floor, and roof may not be plain at all.

You might want to build some basic furnishings for this house. Just put an empty spool into the house and it's a chair. For a more sophisticated chair, make a saw cut just beyond the hole in the spool. Extend the cut a bit beyond the halfway mark. Then saw through the bigger part of the spool until you meet the first saw cut. Another spool makes the pedestal into a kitchen table. Just glue the lid from a jam jar onto the spool. Paint it if you must, but I think the grapes or cherries make a dandy kitchen motif.

Corks make fine furniture. So do popsicle sticks, tiny

matchboxes, plastic or metal film cannisters, spindle spacers, washers and other bits of hardware, old knobs, miniature salt boxes, spice boxes, jar lids...

If you feel like investing the money, you can buy a set of dollhouse furniture at a toy store. Some brands are pretty expensive, but a few of them are made of unpainted wood which children can paint and repaint and paint again. Scraps of plastic or fabric make dandy carpets and wall paper. For super-realists, Con-Tact self-adhesive vinyl in tile or other patterns can create authentic-looking roofs and walls.

DOWN ON THE FARM

You can make your building into a farm simply by taking out the dollhouse equipment and moooving in some farm animals. You can make the animals out of clay (better still, let the kids make them), or you can buy animals ready-made, mold them with plaster molding kits, even carve them out of wood or soap.

For my family's farm, I simply cut out barnyard figures from a beautiful piece of wrapping paper I found downtown one day. If you look around a bit, you'll probably find cards or gift-wrapping paper full of people, animals, and scenes suitable for almost any kind of play building. There are half a dozen ways to mount the cutouts so they stand alone. One of the easiest and surest is to glue them to matching pieces of cardboard as heavy as the bottoms of writing pads. Then slip each mounted cutout into a slit cut into the top of a corrugated cardboard circle or square. Glue will make the figure stand up permanently.

Figure VII-6. The "house" can serve as a farm as well. These people and animals were cut from gift-wrapping paper and glued onto thin cardboard

You don't have to bother cutting around the outsides of all the figures. As you can see in the nearby photo, I left the cutouts squared off. They may look a bit artificial to you, but only if your imagination has been stopped by our mad drive for what we believe to be superrealism. Try the squared-off cutouts on your own children and see if they don't find the scenes plenty "realistic."

GARAGE

A garage is also simple to create out of our building. Just move out most of the furniture or cows and move in the autos. Maybe Junior and Sis would like a hydraulic lift so their mechanics can work comfortably under the cars? If you've built the wooden cars described earlier, simply drill a hole in the bottom of every car to match the top of a clothespin. Then mount one or two ordinary clothespins into an upright position somewhere in the garage. Perch a disabled car atop the clothespin and it'll seem like a very authentic hydraulic lift. If you want to accommodate just any old car, glue a flat piece of wood or cardboard onto the top of your clothespin lift.

More Real Estate

Other uses for this building will depend on your own imagination or your children's. Here are just a few that come to my mind.

How about a grocery store? Children can improvise shelves and counters from small cardboard boxes, empty magnetic tape cassette boxes, scrap lumber, and other odds and ends. You can make hundreds of "tin" cans by sawing $\frac{1}{4}$" to $\frac{1}{2}$" dowels into sundry lengths. You and/or the children can "label" them with colored marking pens.

Some toy stores sell relatively inexpensive sets of miniature food packages. You might want to study them for style, or add a set for a deluxe look.

Would you like a school? Make plenty of the sitting people described later in this chapter, but include some standing models, too. Benches or desks are made from boxes, cardboard, empty spools, sticks, and any of the other materials described earlier for household furniture. You might even want to cut up a "Magic Slate" so the schoolhouse has working blackboards.

There's no reason why this structure shouldn't be used as a castle for children who have medieval toys or minds, as a space platform to go with satellites and space-ships, as a library, ranch, or circus tent for a four-ring circus. Imagination is such a precious thing, and a fragile one. Nurture it by encouraging your children to suggest even the wildest uses for this "Building for All Reasons."

PEOPLE, PEOPLE, PEOPLE

You can certainly find plenty of scale-model people in toy stores. Many of them will work just fine in this building. But why bother? First, the good ones are kind of expensive. Besides, building your own people is fun.

Grab a handful of common wooden clothespins (the ones without the fancy springs), find some scrap lumber or corrugated cardboard (unless you have some spindle spacers on hand), take the glue bottle, locate where you last laid down the saw, and make your own people. A small drill can be useful, and you might want to collect some dowels, straws, wire, or pencils, too.

The clothespin already comes with a well-shaped head, two legs, and a body (see Figure VII-5). That's enough realism for many kids. If you want to add arms, use pieces of ¼″ or 3/16″ dowels, soda-pop straws, or pencils. Fit them into holes drilled in the sides of each clothespin "body." Glue makes the job permanent. Don't stick the arms straight out, or your people will all look like scarecrows!

You can make bendable arms without much puttering. Invest in a couple of feet of ordinary insulated electrical wire, the type used in buildings to wire switches and appliances. Try to buy size #12, but the next smaller or larger size is OK.

To avoid setting up racial identity in the clothespin people, I try to find wire with tan-colored insulation, but that's kind of tough to find these days except in a very well stocked electrical supply company. Red isn't too hard to find, and that's my next choice, although black and white are the most common colors.

Snip the wire into pieces, each about 4″ long. Drill a hole in each clothespin, just big enough for the wire to slip through. Glue generally isn't required. With a pliers, bend each end of the wire into a small loop. That's a *hand!* It's also an ideal way to keep the two ends of wire securely tucked out of harm's way. Once you've exerted enough elbow grease with your pliers to twist those very stiff wires into tight loops, you'll feel confident that little fingers aren't going to untwist them. However, little fingers *will* be able to bend the "arms" at will, putting up the arms, folding them, stretching them out...

You can make the clothespin people stand up by gluing each of them to a slice of closet pole. To make stronger people for rougher kids, chisel or drill slots into the base for the legs. The glue plus the slots make for a very strong support. Alternatively, shape the bottom of each person to fit the hole in a spindle spacer.

Clothespin people really don't need faces. But if you want to add them, it's easy. A red felt-tip pen or ballpoint pen makes lips; a black pen makes eyes, hair, and a nose. If you draw the hair a bit long, you've got a unisex person. (Note: Eyes are in *the middle* of your head, not near the top!)

I wouldn't try to make blue eyes, green eyes, brown eyes, black hair, brown hair, or blond hair. Likewise, I wouldn't try to create white, yellow, red, brown, black, or any other color faces. Let your children play with people just as people.

8 *Puzzles and more puzzles*

If sometimes *you* have trouble getting organized, think how much trouble it must be for youngsters who have relatively few years of experience in making sense out of their world. Puzzles can encourage children to learn the visual and cerebral skills that help them organize the world around them. Loosely used, they can also encourage impromptu editorializing about the world as seen through the eyes of your children.

A puzzle is really nothing more than a picture—only the picture has been broken up arbitrarily. The child who puts the pieces together successfully is rewarded with an unbroken view of some—let's hope—interesting part of the world. The more interesting the picture, the more likely a

Figure VIII-1. Puzzles should be more amusing than puzzling— and that goes double for their construction

child is to go through the mental and physical work required to assemble the disorganized puzzle.

If you and your children make the puzzles together, that extra effort will make the pictures just that much more interesting, and the children will accept the puzzle-working challenge more readily. In addition, a child who begins with an all-together picture can be more confident that it'll go back together again than the child who is simply handed a store-bought puzzle and then told to dump out the pieces and fit them together.

Children are ready for puzzles by the age of two or three. With these homemade puzzles, they may become interested a bit sooner and retain interest in them longer. Older kids (maybe up to 40 or 50), will keep their interest if you're game to make bigger, more complicated versions, even puzzles within puzzles. More about those later.

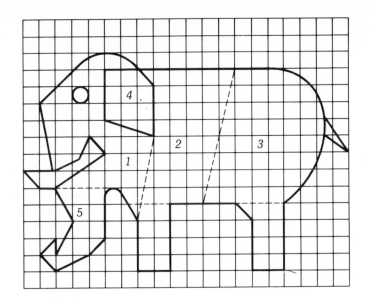
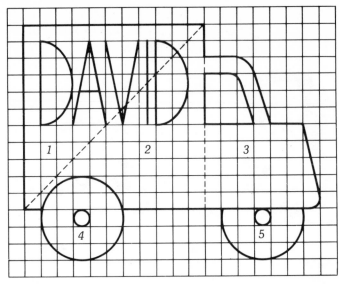

Figure VIII-2. Patterns for the Elephant and Truck Puzzles. Use ½" squares

SIMPLE WOODEN PUZZLES

Simple puzzles for 2- and 3-year-old children are best made from ⅛″ or ¼″ Masonite, or ¼″ plywood. All are readily available from lumberyards and do-it-yourself centers. I prefer the plywood, although commercial puzzles are generally made from Masonite.

For the toddlers, you have to build the puzzle within its own frame. That means you make a tray out of a plain sheet of plywood (or Masonite), cut the puzzle pieces from a second piece of plywood, then glue the border of the puzzle layer onto the bottom layer, forming a three-dimensional frame that holds the pieces neatly in place for clumsy little hands.

For the very young, it's best to start with puzzles that have only two or three pieces. The truck, elephant, teddy bear, abstract parent and child, and child standing on its head shown in nearby figures are especially suitable. Each of them can be cut into just two or three pieces at first. Then, when Junior gets older and better at working puzzles, you can take out the saw again and cut them into more and more complicated works of puzzle art.

Using plywood or Masonite about 8″ x 10″ or 9″ x 12″, start by drawing ½″ squares. Then, following the lines and squares in our sketch, copy whichever shape you like onto your wood. If you prefer, you can draw these puzzles onto paper and then trace them onto wood with carbon paper.

For beginning puzzlers, cut the elephant into pieces number 1 through 3. Later you can cut out pieces number 4 and 5.

The truck has 3 pieces to begin with. Later cut out the wheels for pieces number 4 and 5.

Teddy Bear begins with four pieces—the head, the body, and both arms. Later make it more complex by cutting out the two feet. Still later, cut out the ears.

The flower is more complicated than it may seem. All four petals are identical, or close to it. For beginners, make the top two petals and the center as a single piece. The bottom two petals, pieces 2 and 3, are interchangeable. Later you can separate the top two petals from the center, making a five-piece puzzle. Still later you can add leaves, making even more pieces.

Parent and child separate naturally into three pieces. If you want to, later you can cut each piece in two.

The child standing on its head separates neatly into three pieces—body, head, and arm. Later you can divide the body in two, cut the foot into a separate piece, and even divide the hand from the arm.

In cutting out the puzzle pieces, remember to preserve the outer edges of wood since you'll want to glue those onto the bottom layer. The easiest way is to drill a small hole along one line, then insert your coping or sabre-saw blade. Or, if you're adept at it, you can tilt your sabre saw, turn on the motor, and then slowly bring the tilted blade down onto the wood along one of the straighter lines. That way, the blade begins its own cut. Practice this technique on scrap lumber before trying it on good wood.

Sandpaper the edges of every wooden piece. Don't get carried away with the sanding, or you'll create gaps in the puzzle. But do sand away noticeably rough edges that

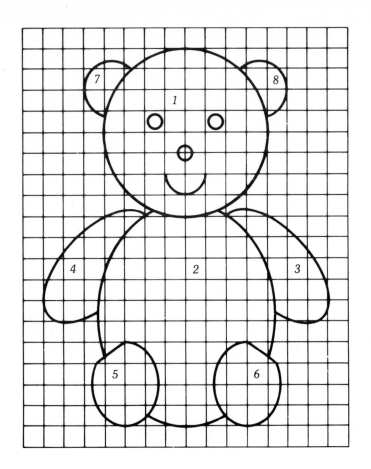

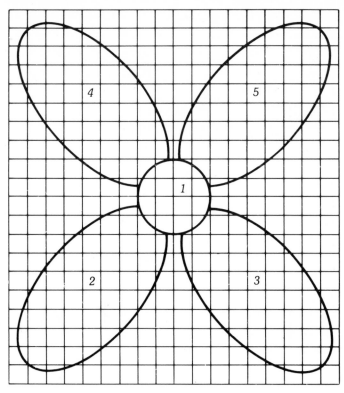

Figure VIII-3. Patterns for Teddy Bear and Flower Puzzles. Use ½" squares

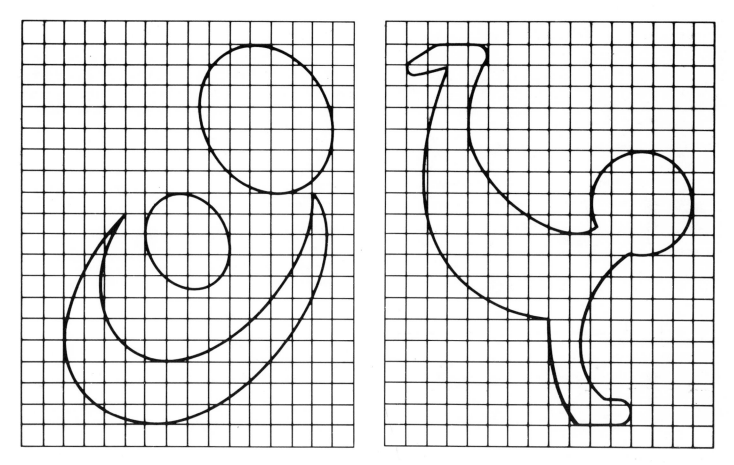

Figure VIII-4. Patterns for the more abstract Parent & Child and Headstand Puzzles. Use ½" squares

can catch on little fingers or detract from the beauty of your puzzle.

After all the pieces are ready, glue your outside "frame" piece to the plain bottom "tray." Use Elmer's Glue-All or a similar product. After the glue dries, smooth off the irregular outside edges with sandpaper, SurForm tool, or saw.

Then lay the pieces into the frame and paint your puzzle. Any rugged nontoxic paint will work nicely.

"PICTURE" PUZZLES

(3 to 6 to play with; 6 to 10 to paint.)
Skills: Easy, but careful sawing is required. Not an ideal first project.
Materials: 8" x 10" or 9" x 12" pieces of thin Masonite or plywood.

Higher up the hardness ladder come these picture puzzles that are made from real pictures. They are most fun when the pictures are of some person or some scene with which the youngster can identify. How about an ethnic hero? A character out of a storybook? Or a photo of the youngster? How about an enlargement of the lake or mountains that highlighted a vacation? Maybe even the cabin or tent itself?

Alternatively, you can clip pictures out of a magazine, collect those large museum postcards showing great works of art, or if you have an artistic side, create your own work

Figure VIII-5. Kevin's puzzle is uniquely personalized—it has his own picture on it!

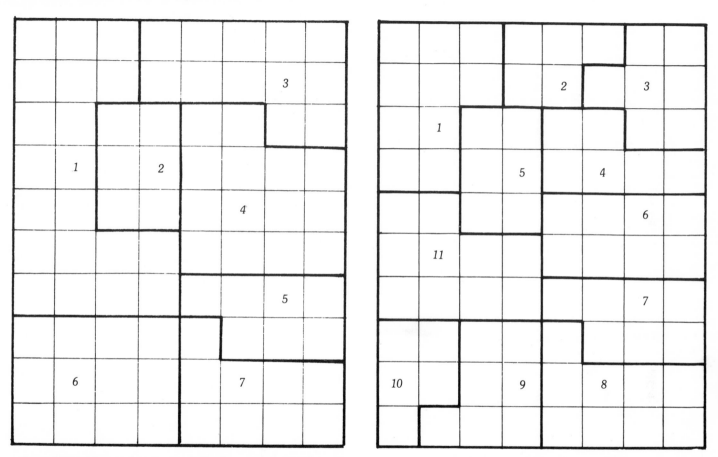

Figure VIII-6. Here and on the two following pages are basic patterns for picture puzzles. (It's simply not as much fun, nor as much of a challenge, if all a youngster's puzzles feature the same pattern.) Use the simpler left-hand designs for easier puzzles, the more complex right-hand versions for older children.

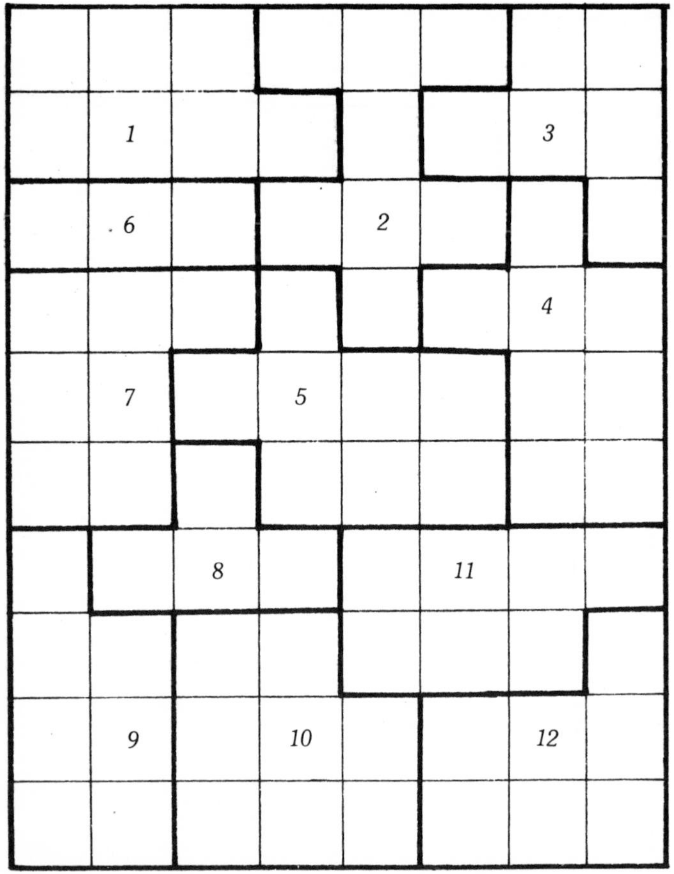
1
3
6
2
4
7
5
8
11
9
10
12

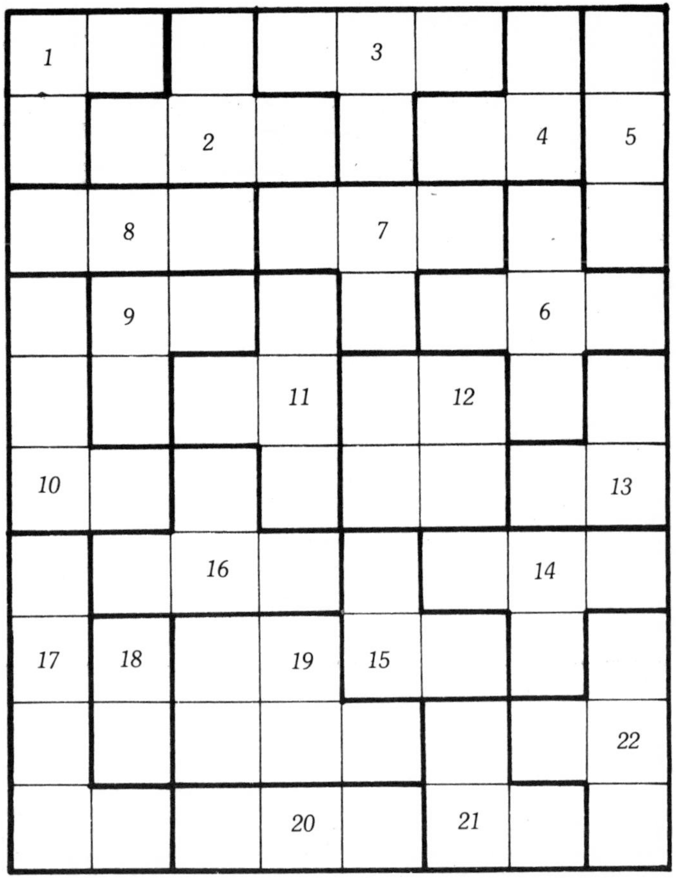
1
3
2
4
5
8
7
9
6
11
12
10
13
16
14
17
18
19
15
22
20
21

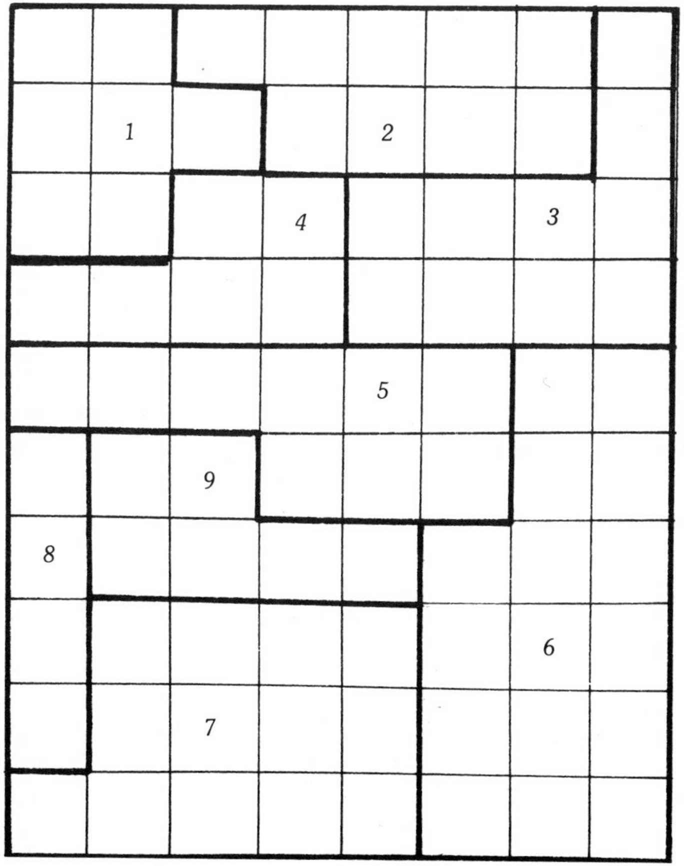
1
2
3
4
5
6
7
8
9

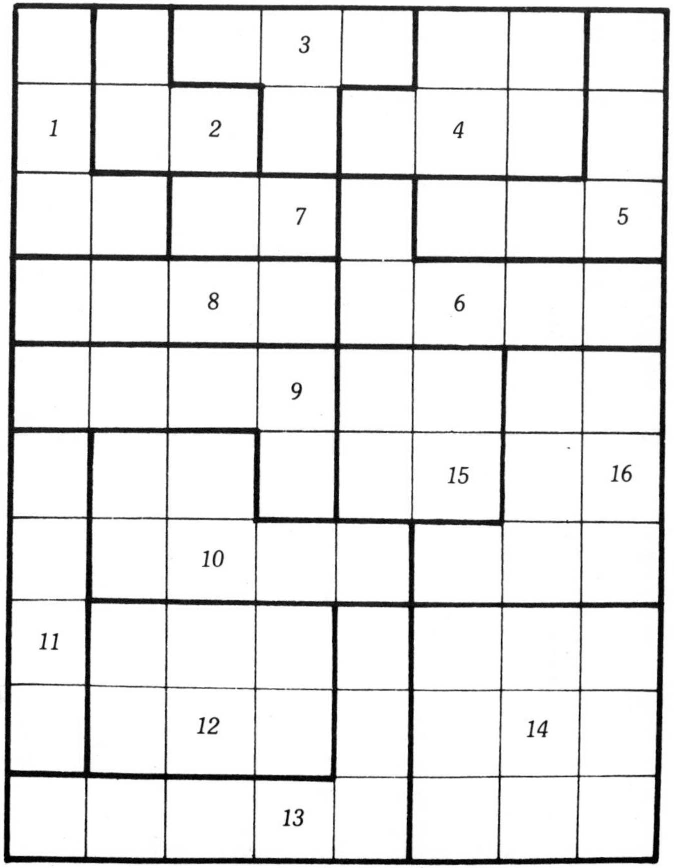
1
2
3
4
5
6
7
8
9
10
11
12
13
14
15
16

of art on Masonite or plywood for conversion into a puzzle. Provide pieces of Masonite and paints for junior artists, and when one of their paintings turns out to be truly superb, maybe you'll want to convert it into a puzzle.

Ordinary Elmer's Glue-All and similar products work nicely for pasting paper pictures onto plywood or Masonite. Apply a generous but not sloppy layer to both the picture and back of the board. Smooth the picture carefully onto the wood. Then weight the two surfaces together with books, bricks, or carpenter's clamps.

A photo or paper picture glued totally to Masonite is unbelievably tough. You may want to varnish or lacquer the surface of the picture to protect it while you work on the puzzle, but if you've glued the picture well, this really isn't required.

Choose one of the three picture puzzle patterns from Figure VIII-6. All three patterns have both a simple and a complicated version. The more complex puzzle is more appropriate for children above the age of 4.

Draw 1" squares on the back of your puzzle-to-be. Then copy your chosen puzzle pattern, using the squares to guide you. When that's done, carefully cut along the lines. The finer-toothed the blade you use on your saw, the finer a puzzle you'll have. Even with a fine blade, it may be necessary to sandpaper the edges lightly.

If you want, you can build these picture puzzles into their own "frame" as with the earlier puzzles. If you draw the shape of the puzzle pieces onto the bottom tray, young children can work the puzzle with ease. It's also easier to store the puzzle if it has its own frame. Taking away the frame later on will provide new challenges—it will make the puzzle harder to work and harder to put away at the end of a long play day. Both of those are good disciplines for growing children.

FROG AND RABBIT PUZZLES

(3 to 6 to play with; 12 and up to build.)
Skills: A little bit demanding. You should be confident of your sawing accuracy.
Materials: 1" pine boards of various sizes.

At first glance, these simple animals seem to make simple puzzles. But even though there are relatively few pieces, the shapes and placements are so similar that young minds have to struggle a bit to reassemble the frog and the rabbit.

The major learning experience from these puzzles comes in figuring out where the various parts of the body go. The rabbit's head, for instance, could possibly go where the tail fastens on. It would give the poor rabbit a stooped back, of course, and that's what Junior has to learn. The left ear and right ear could be interchanged also. The ears themselves *are* the same shape—or as close to the same shape as your hand cutting can make them—but the holes that link ears to head are different.

In the frog, differences between the head holes and the leg holes are subtle indeed. If you do your sawing very carefully, the head and the legs might be interchangeable. But if the head went into one of the leg holes, Sis would end up with a lopsided frog.

Let your children work out these subtleties themselves. Some days, maybe when things haven't gone well,

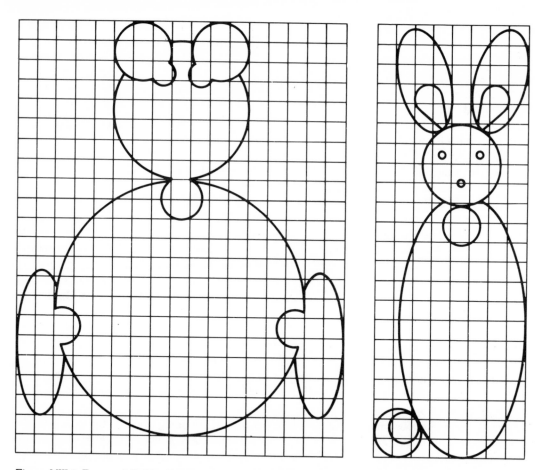

Figure VIII-7. Frog and Rabbit Puzzles are cut from wood after respective designs are sketched onto a grid of ½" squares

Sis may *want* a lopsided figure to help work out whatever's bothering her. Besides, kids need a chance to get back occasionally at that Big, Mysterious, sometimes Frightening Outside World. Flexible puzzles like these, along with flexible parents and teachers, can provide an outlet.

These animals look nicest when cut from 1" pine or hardwood. Masonite or plywood is OK, though. As shown, the frog requires an 8½" wide board. If that's tough to find locally, get an 8" board (actually only 7½" wide) and reduce the ½" squares in my original drawing to only 7/16" or 3/8".

Seal the lumber unpainted and unstained, if you choose, according to battle plans drawn up in earlier chapters. If colors turn you on—or if you're hoping they turn on Junior—you can make a green frog and a pink bunny, a pink frog and a green bunny, or whatever you and the kids fancy.

Storing your puzzles

Puzzle pieces have a bad habit of jumping out of their proper location and mixing together. As children get older, they can be given responsibility for taking care of their own puzzles. This can include figuring out, pretty much on their own, how to keep the pieces from the various puzzles separated. You might suggest that they sew small cloth bags, one for each puzzle. Or save up boxes from cigars, cheese, books, and such for the kids to paint or cover with Con-Tact vinyl plastic using a distinctive color or pattern for each puzzle box. (It's amazing how well even very young children can associate a color or a pattern with a particular toy.)

Here's a hint that will help little tykes sort out the pieces after they've mysteriously merged—as they always do. Paint the backs of the pieces of every separate puzzle a different color. By flipping the pieces over, youngsters can sort out quickly which pieces belong to which puzzle. If they are old enough, use an identifying number or letter applied with magic marker.

LACING BOARDS

(3 to 6 to play with; 6 to 10 to make.)
Skills: Extremely easy.
Materials: 8" x 10" pieces of pegboard.

Lacing boards are very much like puzzles. Besides, I like to make them from the same pictures as some of the simple puzzles, so I'm going to include them in this chapter.

Basically the lacing board is a picture with holes in it that youngsters can "sew" with a hefty piece of "thread." In our case, as with many commercially produced lacing boards, the thread will be big, colorful shoelaces. I prefer the heavy kind that's used in boots or full-sized tennis shoes; and the brighter the better.

Lacing boards work wonders for coordination. They give fingers a chance to push large shoestrings into tiny holes over and over again. Every time the fingers and eyes successfully coordinate in lacing another hole, the picture looks better and better. When all of the *desired* holes are filled, the child instantly sees what a beautiful picture his

Figure VIII-8. If a lacing board is used with pegs (or golf tees, as shown here in Oscar's hands) it becomes a picture pegboard

struggles have created. I stress *desired holes* because some kids won't want to fill up the picture the same way you or I might fill it. In fact, *you* might not fill it the way *I* would. We're all beautifully different people and always will be. *You* can encourage Sis to fill up more and more of the lacing-board holes, but if *I* wanted to show off what more laces look like in a lacing board, I'd lace it myself!

Lacing boards aren't hard to make. Start out with some 8″ x 10″ or 9″ x 12″ pieces of ⅛″ or ¼″ pegboard. The thinner variety is definitely preferred. Most lumberyards and do-it-yourself centers sell the stuff in odd-sized pieces, so you won't have to buy a full 4′ x 8′ sheet unless you plan to make a few dozen lacing boards for a classroom or as gifts.

Turn back to the drawings for the simple puzzles— Figures VIII-2 to VIII-4. Using the pegboard holes as guides for your grid markings, sketch the elephant and friends onto pegboards. Get out some paints and do them up neatly—but not too brightly, please. Many of the store-bought lacing boards look like circus scenes. My own feeling, seconded by the child-development people I consulted for this book, is that the figures ought to be a bit subdued. The child should *add the brightness* by sewing the brightly colored threads into the boards.

At first Sis will simply lace the shoestring in and out of the outline, all along the perimeter of the truck, flower, etc. That's why I recommend that you paint only the figure itself, not the background. Leave that the dull brown of the pegboard.

But the real fun is in using pegboard, with all its holes, for your project. Later, probably after Sis passes the 4- or 5-year-old mark, she'll be able to add to the lacing figure's complexity. Perhaps she'll lace her name on the truck in one color, do the outline in another, cover the wheels entirely in one color, and the body in still another color. At that point, you'll want to have plenty of different-colored shoestrings!

PEGBOARDS

(Age 4 to 7 to play with.)

We've already discussed how to make a set of pegboards into which children lace multihued shoestrings, forming three-dimensional scenes while sharpening their coordination. You just didn't know that when we discussed how to create lacing boards, the same boards double as pegboards. All you need are pegs.

You can make pegs out of dowels that match the holes in your boards—generally about ⅛″ or 3/16″—and spend a whole evening coloring them. Or you can buy them ready-made at a good toy store. Or you can go to the nearest sport shop and invest a buck in a bag of golf tees. They fit nicely into the holes and aren't sharp enough at their tips to worry me. (If they worry you, five minutes with sandpaper will fix that.) They're also colorful and have built-in handles to boot! Another feature in using tees is that this shows kids how locally available materials make great toys.

Figure VIII-9. Viz Lit-II Puzzle, a challenging exercise for the curious and creative

VISUAL LITERACY PUZZLE-I

(8 and up to play with or build.)
Skills: Easy.
Materials: Miscellaneous pictures, cardboard, glue.

Visual literacy ("Viz Lit" for short) puzzles are tools for older kids (and adults, too) to use in making their own unique graphic statements about how they'd like to organize the world around them. I've used them in puzzle-sized formats for individual children to create with, used them in giant-sized displays for multimedia happenings, and seen them assembled for projections big enough to fill an auditorium.

Basically, Viz Lit puzzles start with *sets* of photographs, pictures lifted from magazines, calendar pictures, works of art, or any similar graphic material. Accumulating a matched set is a little tricky until you get the knack, but it's well worth working on. First, the set generally works best if it has a common theme—buildings, people standing up, people's full faces, people doing things.... Added to that, you generally want similar objects in similar places in every one of the pictures in a set. Here's why.

When Junior gets a Viz Lit puzzle, there's no "right" or "wrong" way to assemble it. If he happens to feel like putting a clown's head on a cop's body on a fat lady's legs, that's fine. On the other hand, if he's in a more docile mood, he might want the clown's head on a clown's body on top of a clown's legs. It'll fit together either way, unlike the classic puzzles where every piece has a specific, correct place.

Cut each of the individual pictures into thirds. If you're the orderly type, at the start you can make each section a different height: the third that includes heads can be relatively short, the third that includes bodies can be taller, and the bottom third can be tallest of all. That way, Junior will tend to put heads on top, bodies in the middle, and legs at the bottom.

If Junior's already sophisticated enough, you can begin immediately by making all of the sections—top, middle, bottom—the same size. Or you can move on to that aspect when you're secure in the other. It's now entirely possible that Junior will stack three heads on top of each other, and alongside that three pairs of legs atop one another, followed by stomachs.

We're not limited to people. Viz Lit puzzles can be made up of animals, buildings, landscapes; you name it. After you've started your collection, the children will find as many pictures to add to the set as you will!

Glue your Viz Lit puzzle pictures onto something heavy. Best material of all is ⅛" Masonite. Plywood, chipboard, heavy cardboard, and similar substances work well, too. All of the pictures have to be trimmed to the same size. Then you can make the uniform cuts, turning a single picture into three or four pieces of a Viz Lit puzzle.

VIZ LIT PUZZLE-II

(4 and up to play with; 8 and up to build.)
Skills: Very easy, but some patience is helpful.
**Materials: Miscellaneous pictures and forty-eight 1"
cubes.**

An extension of the idea formulated in Viz Lit-I, this puzzle expands to a three-dimensional set of pictures. It's more complex than Viz Lit-I, but it doesn't require as much constant adding to to keep young minds enthralled.

Because I'm lazy, I built my Viz Lit-II puzzle out of forty-eight pieces of 1″ plastic cubes, but they're kind of expensive. You can make your cubes out of wood or Styrofoam plastic. With luck or persistence, you might be able to find some ready-made out of wood or cardboard.

Then I located four photographs that had subject matter complicated enough to lend themselves to being broken up into forty-eight parts. Working on one picture at a time, I cut each picture into forty-eight separate pieces and glued them onto the forty-eight cubes. I arranged the picture parts carefully, however, so that the upper-left-hand corner of the 6″ x 8″ puzzle is the upper-left-hand corner for *all* of the photographs incorporated into the puzzle. In other words, if you have a fully assembled picture on top, if you turn all forty-eight cubes on their right side, you'll again have a fully assembled picture. Likewise if you turn the cubes completely over.

My four photographs took care of only four sides of the six-sided cubes. On one remaining side I put 1″ black and white squares, checkerboard fashion. On the other remaining side I glued squares of colored paper, in no particular order.

To emphasize the 6″ x 8″ format of the Viz Lit-II puzzle, it's a good idea at least to set the pieces onto a 6″ x 8″ board of some sort. To really make it fancy, you can add a narrow frame around the board to contain all of the pieces. The frame helps keep pieces from getting lost in storage.

Many children play with Viz Lit-II by trying to rebuild a complete picture. That means finding which of six sides of each of the forty-eight cubes belongs to the picture in question—and then, jigsaw-puzzle style, where the cube has to be positioned. That can take over an hour!

Many children skip right over the reconstruction phase and begin by editorializing from the beginning. They assemble the cubes into an abstract view, adding black or colored cubes amid the more realistic picture cubes. After turning over the puzzle to your kids with a few words of advice about the possible ways of using it, you can count on never playing with it again yourself, except when the little darlings are asleep.

9 *Do-it-yourself books*

The fact that you've picked up a book and actually read it this far sets you apart from the general population. More than likely, you also want your children to develop an appreciation for books.

That may not be easy to accomplish these days. With the excuse that we're now in a visual era, many schools, parents, and even publishers are turning on TV sets, pointing projectors at screens, and generally bringing up a generation that scarcely knows the value of books.

It's obvious that I am committed to educating children to the importance of our visual world, but I also think it's important to have books in the playroom, the classroom, and everywhere else children spend any time. So let's make some books that are personal, useful, and literate.

BABY'S FIRST BOOK

(6 months to 2 years to play with; 10 years and up to build.)
Skills: Simple sewing skills required or have to be acquired.
Materials: Soft cloth and colored sewing thread or yarn.

Any soft fabric in the hands of mother, father, friends, relatives, or neighbors can become a book. *Fabric* for baby's first book doesn't have to be fancy. Simple cotton or polyester such as is found in bedsheets works nicely. In fact, one old sheet provides enough cloth to sew several books. Pages should be approximately 8" by 10".

Books for infants don't need words. Pictures alone are just fine. I'd like to see people making their own decisions as to what they want to see in baby's first books. Don't let the Madison Avenue penchant for the glossy and the super-real influence you. Let the simplified, more primitive art of a Grandma Moses, a Picasso, or the neighborhood children guide your standards. If you feel much more comfortable copying pictures than locating your own, then copy mine from the chapter on puzzles and lacing boards. The teddy bear, truck, child on his hands, and other designs make nice book pages. In fact, why not make several of the flowers, each one in entirely different colors? Figure on from four to eight pictures in a book.

There are endless ways to apply the colorful pictures to the cloth pages of your books. One of the following methods should fit nicely into your own interests and capabilities.

Embroidery is a lovely technique to use for a child's book. Using your favorite embroidery method, stitch pictures onto half a dozen or so pages with yarns of your choice. Then put any two pages back to back and hem together three of their edges—top, bottom, and one side. Try to make the hems uniform so that the completed pages come out identical sizes.

Lay the pages together carefully. Then, over the unhemmed edges, wrap a 2″ wide strip of cloth turned under ¼″ at its edges. I prefer to see some bright color used there. Stitch the cloth to the pile of pages. Either make a double row of stitches, or zigzag the entire length of the strip. Even babies have enough strength to pull loose any carelessly stitched books.

Appliqué is a second way of sewing colorful cloth books. Trace the various designs onto bright scraps of fabric, and then cut and stitch them onto your pages to form simple shapes out of colorful cloth: squares, circles, triangles, even stars. Hem and bind the appliquéd book just like the embroidered version.

If you're ambitious, you can copy some of my puzzle designs or some pictures of your own choosing. By picking contrasting colors or prints in your fabric, you can make striking flowers, teddy bears, trucks, and so on.

You can paint cloth book pages too. I wouldn't recommend textile paints or any other commercially available materials—babies love to chew on their cloth books, and I can't begin to check the safety of the contents of the dozens of brand-name paints on the market. But your kitchen probably has a set of "paints" on hand—U.S. government-certified food colors.

Even though they have been in use for generations, there's some legitimate doubt about the *total* safety of food colorings in food. I don't add any of the stuff to cakes I'm baking or foods I'm cooking. However, the very tiny amounts a baby might get from a piece of cloth, even one that's sucked on all day, are OK in my book. But that's a decision you're going to have to make for yourself.

Painting on cloth with food colors isn't like painting on canvas or paper. If you put a lot of the liquid onto your brush, it spreads out quickly in all directions. I suggest that, after you've traced a design onto your cloth page, you start near the middle of an area and work slowly toward the boundaries. Near the edge of any colored area use as dry a brush as possible.

By using vinegar, you can kill two birds with that one proverbial stone. Moisten your cloth pages with it before starting to paint with food colors. The moisture keeps the dyes from spreading so fiercely, and the vinegar helps to *fix* the color, to make it less prone to rubbing off later on.

Let the pages become almost dry, and then iron them. The heat helps to fix the colors even more. If any of the vinegary odor remains, you can get rid of it by quickly soaking the page in a minimum amount of water and then quickly wringing it all out. The soaking and other handling of these pages will make the colors run a bit, but if you glance at the work of Van Gogh, Picasso, Chagall, and many other major painters, you'll find that their colors aren't kept inside neat coloring-book lines either!

Since the food coloring soaks right through your pages, you'll end up with the same picture on both sides of the cloth. You *could* use the pages as they are, therefore. But I prefer hemming two of them together as we talked about earlier. Either way, sew the pages together to form your finished book.

Covers

Baby will never know whether the book has a cover, much less that books are *supposed* to have covers. But if you're embarrassed about what the neighbors might think, you can paint, appliqué, or embroider a cover. I'll even go along with the admittedly silly convention by providing lettering and design for your cover in Figure IX-1.

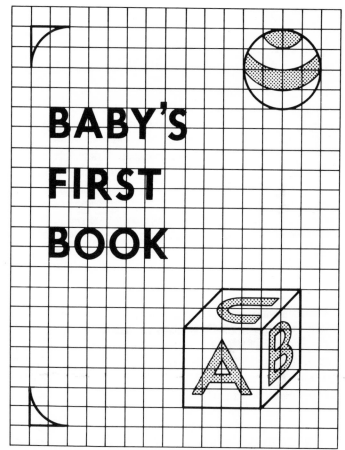

Figure IX-1. "Baby's First Book" can have a fancy cover if you copy this pattern—or one of your own—onto your project. Using Con-Tact plastic, you can create an almost indestructible book with photographs, memorabilia, and natural objects as "illustrations"

PLASTIC BOOKS

(2 years and up to use; 10 years and up to make.)
Skills: Very easy.
Materials: Self-adhesive vinyl and lots of pictures.

You can use transparent Con-Tact plastic to turn almost any series of pictures, photographs, drawings, writings, leaves, cutouts, or other materials into rugged, cleanable books. They're so inexpensive that you can create a new book every time the children pick up a new interest.

After a vacation, before a holiday, during a special event—any time's the right time to make a book. Besides providing a permanent record of a significant occasion, putting a child's pictures or snapshots or other memorabilia into book form gives them the importance they deserve. The fact that these plastic-covered book pages are tough, waterproof, and can be scrubbed makes them ideal for young children who are prone to rip out, tear, or spill on the traditional paper scrapbooks.

Assemble all of the illustrations you or the children want for each book. The pictures, leaves, sketches, and such do not all have to be the same size. However, if the material runs much larger than 8″ x 10″, the book can become unwieldy unless you work very carefully. For your first project, I wouldn't advise your tackling a book that large.

When you become experienced in working with self-adhesive plastics, you'll be able to cut the transparent plastic exactly to size. For each page in your book, use one sheet of plastic that lies over the top of the page from left to right, then folds over onto itself at the right edge (sticky side to sticky side), then lies on the underside of the page, leaving at least an inch of excess at the left side for binding the pages together later. For starters, cut your plastic like this:

> Width: double the width of your biggest picture and add 2″
> Height: add 2″ to the height of your biggest picture.

For each page you plan to create, lay two pictures back-to-back. A dab of glue or strip of tape will hold them together while you work. Then lay your Con-Tact plastic over the top picture carefully so its left half will cover it. Leaving an inch at the right, fold the plastic over and sandwich the bottom picture to the top. Smooth out both sides. If small air bubbles have accumulated, poke a hole with knife or scissors, smooth the bubbles out, and the tiny hole will never be noticed.

If you're working with pictures that are grossly different in size, insert a standard-sized piece of paper between them. You can include coins, leaves, and other thin objects of that sort in books like these. If a view of both sides of the object is valuable, simply lay it onto the appropriate place on a sheet of plastic and sandwich it into a page.

After all of the pages are covered with plastic, trim them to a uniform size on three sides. Don't trim the side that gets bound into the book. Since the plastic has to hold each page together, be sure to leave at least ½″ margin of plastic showing all around the picture.

Now get out your iron and heat it up. In the meantime, square up all the edges of your book's pages. Then double over the plastic on your binding size. Cover the binding edge completely with aluminum foil. Don't be stingy—this is a temporary cover to keep melting plastic from sticking to your iron or the ironing board. With your iron at its hottest setting, slowly and firmly iron along the binding edge to melt the plastic, fusing it together. Be sure to flip the book over so you can iron on both sides of the book's binding. Then remove the aluminum foil. The resulting smooth bead of fused plastic makes a neat and permanent book binding.

When you're involved in book making with children under about 6 or 8 years old, you'll have to do the ironing yourself. Over that age, many children can handle the iron without danger as long as adults supervise and assist, but ask yourself whether you really want to risk the family iron.

The same approximate cut-off ages apply to handling the Con-Tact plastic. There's no danger in using that, but it requires a fair amount of dexterity to apply successfully. When in doubt, let the kids try it. If it gets too frustrating, most will gladly relinquish total responsibility for the easier job of acting as helpers.

QUICKIE PLASTIC-COVERED BOOKS

(8 years and up to play with and to build.)
Skills: Extremely easy, even for 30-year-olds.
Materials: Writing paper and plastic page binders.

For home and classroom projects of all sorts, older children can assemble pictures, stories, and other treasures into books within minutes. The secret? Clear plastic binders. They're inexpensive, versatile, easy to use, and reusable.

You don't have to punch holes in your pages to use these binders. Therefore, some eager young hands pulling on a page can't damage it. If somebody does pull too hard, the page simply slips out of the book, and you can slip it right back in. And unlike the pages of conventional scrapbooks, these are relatively easy to change around at will. The instructions that come with every binder are amazingly straightforward. You can cram up to fifty standard pieces of typing paper into one binder.

To show that neatness sometimes pays, parents or teachers might consider buying some plastic page binders and working with the kids in getting all of their maps, instructions, special pictures, or mementoes into book form. Red-edged binders might be for vacation memories, yellow for collections, blue for Scout activities, and green for miscellaneous pictures that may not have immediate purpose but are too valuable to toss out.

In these days when the art of communicating on paper seems to be dying out, I like to encourage kids to take an interest in making written presentations in any way possible. One exciting way is with transfer letters and transfer art. You can buy them in art stores or stationery stores that cater to advertising personnel or commercial artists. Most brands cost a couple of dollars per sheet. One sheet of ½" tall letters is generally enough to design a dozen professional-looking title pages. Professional, mechanical, electrical, artistic, architectural and scientific symbols, arrows, numbers, and other printing devices are also supplied in transfer sheets.

To use transfer letters, first sketch your sample cover layout lightly in pencil. Draw a light, straight pencil line across the page ⅛" below each line of letters you want. Locate the center of the page and the center letter in each line of type. Lay the appropriate letter into the appropriate spot on your cover (or other page), and rub firmly over the letter with a dull pencil point or ballpoint pen point. Like magic, the letter transfers from the plastic sheet onto your page. Then move on to your next letter. It takes more time to explain this process than it will take you to do it.

10 *Toys you can count on*

Let's face it, numbers are pretty important in our children's lives. They can learn about numbers in all sorts of different ways. On TV they may watch "Sesame Street" to learn counting. Or they may learn about numbers from TV shows and TV commercials that teach how to count stolen money, corpses, crummy prize offerings, and raisins in the cereal bowl.

You can take your chances, or you can take the matter into your own hands and start developing your own materials with which to get kids started working with numbers—at the same time passing on your personal ideas about what things we should count.

FLIPPING BEADS

(6 months to 2 years to play with; 10 years and up to build.)
Skills: Easy. A good first project.
Materials: Small scrap of wood, #12 insulated wire, miscellaneous "beads."

This set of beads on a flexible loop is one of the earliest homemade toys you can spring on your youngsters, and a simple first toy for adults or older youngsters to build. The Flipping Beads are colorful and encourage manipulation with the hands. As baby gets older and stronger, the loop can be twisted into different contours.

Start with a wooden base. You can use a simple 5" circle or a square piece from a 6" board. Use 1" pine, ¾" or

½″ plywood, chipboard, or any similar building material. Cut carefully and then use a SurForm tool or sandpaper to thoroughly round and smooth all of the edges. You don't want baby's fingers or mouth to pick up splinters.

The loop is fashioned from a 24″ piece of #12 insulated electrical wire. You can buy it at hardware, electrical, or building supply outlets. The insulation most commonly available is black, white, tan, and red. I prefer the red, but any other color will work just fine.

Figure X-2 shows where to drill holes in your base. Choose a drill that is very close to the size of the insulated wire. A $5/32$″ drill worked fine with my toy. If that proves to be too snug, switch to $3/16$″. But if you don't have a drill, you can *burn* the holes through wood. Over a gas stove, carefully heat the end of a coat hanger and plunge it into the exact spot where you need a hole. The hot wire will burn part way through the wood. Repeat the process until the hole is burned through completely.

You want to enable the base to sit flat even after wires are run downward through one hole, across the ½″ gap, and then upward through a matching hole. Therefore, you have to gouge out a deep trench measuring almost ¼″ between the pair of holes at each side of the base. You can use a SurForm tool, file, knife, chisel, sandpaper, or any similar tool.

On the Flipping Beads that I built, by the time I twisted that very stiff piece of wire around and shoved it into the inside of the two matching holes, and then

Figure X-1. Dawn is having a ball with this homemade "Flipping Beads" set, made from a length of electrical cable, plus odds and ends

repeated the process on the opposite side of the base with the opposite end of the wire, it seemed very firmly affixed. I have no fears that the wire will work loose. If you want to be extra sure, however, run enough wire through the two holes so that you can neatly wrap the loose end around the foot of the wire loop several times.

"Beads" can be gathered from a variety of sources. I feel the more shapes, the merrier—empty wooden spools of thread, wooden closet-pole supports, spindle spacers, one or more curved segments cut from a shapely spindle. I've gently flattened off four sides of a donut-shaped spindle to make one "bead" for the Flipping Beads. You, too, can cut your own shapes, but they should not be much wider than 2", not much thicker than 1", and they should have ¼" holes through their centers. They have to be sanded smooth.

Six or eight beads is a good number. They should be as colorful as possible. I soaked my wood in food colors. When dry, I sealed in the color with linseed oil. (You can buy linseed oil at most art stores.) Child-proof paints and penetrating wood sealer are supposed to be nontoxic, but I just don't feel like taking a chance on a toy like this that'll spend so much time in baby's mouth.

COUNTING NOSES NUMBER PUZZLE

(4 to 6 to play with; 12 and up to build.)
Skills: Very easy.
Materials: Cardboard and magazine pictures.

For youngsters just getting fascinated by numbers, or for

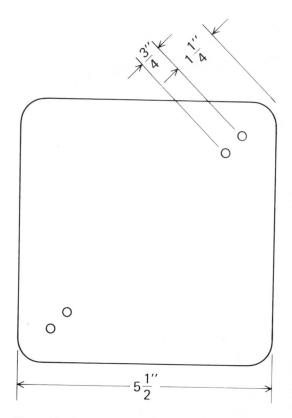

Figure X-2. Pattern for the base of a "Flipping Beads" set

Figure X-3. Part of my own set of "Counting Noses" Puzzles

older kids having problems memorizing numbers, this set of number puzzles makes rote learning a lot more fun. On one half of each puzzle, the child has to count faces. Then he has to find the numeral that goes with that number of faces. Only the puzzle piece that has the correct numeral printed on it will interlock with the card full of faces. If the child has figured correctly, he'll get the instant gratification of knowing that the answer is right. If not, the card full of faces is still there, ready to be counted a second time.

There have been puzzles like this one on the toy and educational markets, but I never much cared for the drab, dumb-looking pictures they all seemed to feature. Aside from that, they all had one major practical problem—their arrangement of slots is too obvious. Any lazy but bright kid who took a moment to study the interlocking slots, rather than count the apples, faces, or whatevers, would not need to learn how to count at all.

In my do-it-yourself version, the slots are so subtle that even kids with sharp visual senses would probably find it easier to count than to study the puzzle shapes. Still, there's no chance for a mix-up because the right number slips in easily. The wrong number won't slip in unless Sis takes a knife to it!

There are twenty number puzzles in this set. You can make them on cardboard you collect from sources such as the backs of writing tablets. But I'd strongly recommend that you buy one 20″ x 30″ sheet of inexpensive illustration board from an art store. Its shiny white surface and durable backing makes a professional-looking job.

Figure X-4. How to lay out the interlocking elements for your own set of "Counting Noses" Puzzles

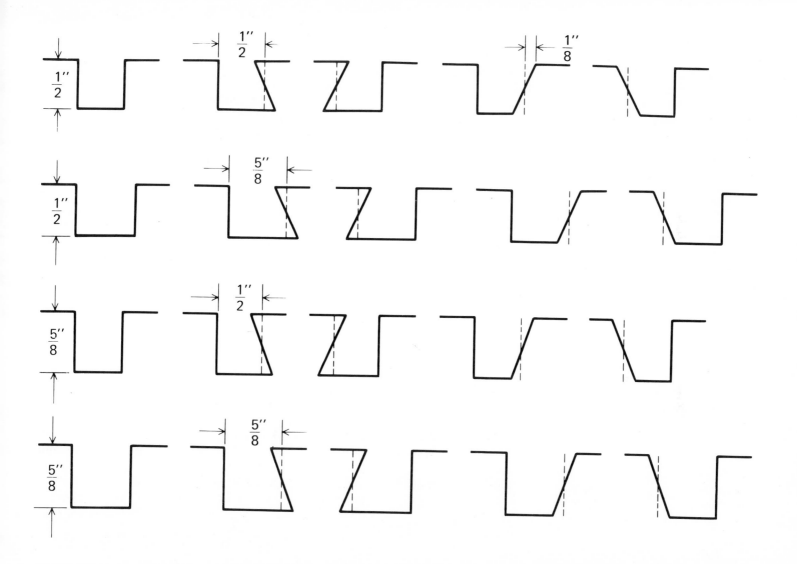

Cut the illustration board into rectangles that are 7½" x 5". You'll be able to get twenty-four of them out of the one illustration board. Use a razor blade or X-Acto knife for cutting, and a metal-edged ruler for guiding the razor blade; you won't be able to get accurate enough cuts with scissors. (For dividing up the board, a paper cutter works fine. Later you'll have to use a knife or razor blade, however.)

Draw a line 1¾" from the bottom of each of twenty rectangles. (Set aside your four extra pieces to back up any errors.) Then, consulting Figure X-4, draw the twenty different interlocking configurations onto your twenty puzzle rectangles. But don't cut them apart just yet.

On the bottom piece of each puzzle, draw each number from 1 to 20. If you really want a professional-looking job, invest in a sheet of transfer type (described in the previous chapter) that has numbers about an inch high. (That size type is known as "96 point" in the art and printing trade.) Pick a simple type style, please. Then rub the numerals onto your puzzles.

Now take scissors in hand and head for a pile of old magazines, catalogues, and similar picture-laden publications. Being very people-oriented, I chose to make all twenty puzzle cards with peoples' faces—whites, blacks, Indians, Orientals, youngsters, and senior citizens, men and women, some in blue-collar work clothes and others in white-collar work clothes. The works! Maybe you'd prefer to cut out animals, flowers, cars. You can even choose a different subject for each card. To keep from confusing young minds, in cutting them out, be sure to follow these guidelines:

Include only one face (or other object) per cut-out square (circle cutouts are OK, but you'll probably find cutting squares is easier).

Fill up the square with the object itself; don't include much background in the picture.

Choose your pictures so all the faces (or other objects) on any one puzzle card will be quite uniform in size.

Don't mix black-and-white pictures with color pictures on a card (it's OK to make one card with color, one black and white).

Choose pictures that will allow as much room *between* objects as the objects themselves occupy. (In other words, 1" wide picture squares require about 1" of blank card between them.) Therefore, on the "1" card you can utilize one large picture if you want to, but on the "20" card you'll need twenty small ones.

Now paste down one picture on the "1" puzzle card, two pictures on the "2" card, and so on. Arrange them neatly as you go along. By the time you hit the higher numbers, you'll have to lay out the pictures in advance so you'll know for sure that they all fit.

I like to spray clear plastic over projects like this. If your kids are on the rough side, or the puzzles are for use in schools, they'll last longer if you cover them with transparent self-adhesive plastic.

Cutting apart the twenty puzzle cards takes some patience. First slice carefully around the three sides of each interlocking piece. When that's completed, you can slice on the straight lines. Then you can turn the puzzles over to the budding genius-in-residence.

Start youngsters off with only the first half-dozen cards. When they've learned those numbers, move the limit up to ten, to fifteen, and finally all the way to twenty. Except in unusual circumstances, it seldom pays to use cards for numbers higher than twenty.

ABACUS

(4 and up to play with; 8 and up to build, with adult assistance.)
Skills: Easy to build one. A little tougher to build a beautiful-looking model.
Materials: Beads or spacers, a few scraps of wood, coat hangers.

There is something deliciously humbling about the centuries-old abacus. After you've learned to use it well, you'll outperform anybody using pencil and paper, and it's even possible to figure faster on it than on a pocket calculator!

Keep in mind that the abacus is a *real* calculator. Not only a child, but even an adult can learn how to add or subtract on it with unbelievable speed. In addition, the systematic arrangement of beads vividly teaches the math concepts of a "ones" column, a "tens" column, a "hundreds" column . . . because there actually are columns of beads that represent ones, tens, hundreds, and on up as far as you care to go. For the abacus I've built for this book, I stopped at six columns, which means you can handle numbers up to 999,999. You can add many more columns to this basic abacus.

Figure X-5. A child can count on an abacus more quickly than on his fingers — and use it to add as fast as with pencil and paper

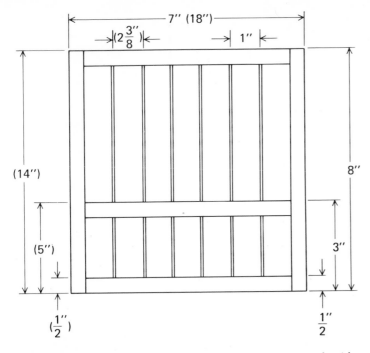

Figure X-6. Dimensions for your own abacus can comply with either set of these: the smaller dimensions (without parentheses) are for an abacus made from beads and coathanger wire. The larger figures (in parentheses) are for the wooden spacer and dowel model. Or, you can come up with your own sizes, using these proportions as your guide

First let's build an abacus; then I'll show you how to use one.

Beads for an abacus can come from all sorts of different sources. *Spindle spacers* are easy to obtain, easy to work with, and look neat. They're a bit large, how-ever—almost 2" in diameter, resulting in an abacus about 14" square. *Stringing beads,* available in hobby and educational toy stores, are often less than ½" in diameter, giving a final result close to 7" square. *Plastic discs,* found in many hobby and plastic stores, come in sundry sizes; some of them have holes through the center, others don't. You need forty-two beads for this abacus, and you might not feel like drilling forty-two holes.

In counting or calculating, you and your children will have to slide the beads toward the center or toward the outside. Large beads, such as spindle spacers, slide on ¼" dowels. The tinier *stringing beads* slide on wires clipped from stiff metal coat hangers. Since both ends of each wire are buried in a very solid wooden frame, I don't consider the wires a hazard at all.

Even though I'm shamelessly in love with the look and feel of natural wood such as spindle spacers, I'll show you how to make an abacus with the smaller colored beads. They're much less expensive, and they make the point.

Here's the list of materials for an abacus made from beads:

Forty-two round beads approximately ½" in dia-meter

Three 1" x 7" strips of ½" plywood

Two 1" x 8" strips of ½" plywood

Six pieces of 7½" wire cut from coat hangers

For an abacus made from spindle spacers, here's the materials list:

Forty-two spindle spacers approximately 2" in diameter

Three 2" x 18" strips of ½" plywood (¾" plywood is OK)

Two 2" by 14" strips of ½" plywood (¾" OK)

1" brads or finishing nails

Six 13½" long, ¼" diameter wooden dowels

Starting with the three boards cut to the same length, mark the location of the six holes. Use Figure X-6 for dimensions.

In the one center board, drill the holes completely through the six locations for rods. On the two end boards, drill your six holes about ¼" deep. The holes in the end boards must be drilled carefully. Your rods are 7½" long, and the space between the two endpieces is 7". That allows each rod to be sunk ¼" into each endpiece. If the holes are a little shallow or the rods a little long, the rods will not fit without bending. On the other hand, the rods can wiggle loose if the holes are too deep. So test your holes as you assemble the abacus.

Using both glue and nails, fasten the sidepieces of the frame to one endpiece. Then fasten the divider (the one with holes drilled all the way through) into place. Don't forget that it isn't supposed to be centered.

Shove each rod in turn through the dividing board and slip on all of the beads, two on the shorter side of the divider and five on the longer side. Then shove the rod into the endpiece that's already fastened into place. After all of the rods and beads are in place, carefully fit the remaining endpiece into location. Glue and nail it.

After SurForming and/or sanding the frame one last time, you can give it a natural finish or paint it. Beads can be colored, painted, or left the way you bought them.

When you turn the abacus over to your youngsters,

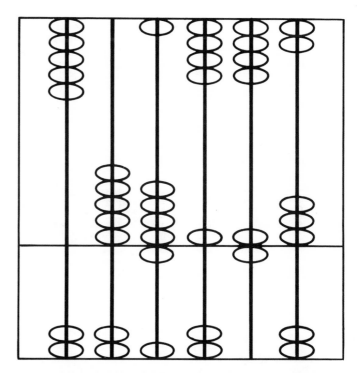

Figure X-7. How to read an abacus: From left to right, the columns stand for 100,000s, 10,000s, 1,000s, 100s, 10s, and then ones. In the far left (100,000s) column, none of the beads are in the center, so read "0". In the 10,000s column, all 5 top beads (each worth 1) are toward the center, but none of the bottom beads (each worth 5) is moved, so read "5". In the 1,000s, one bottom bead and 4 top beads have been moved; thus, "9". And so forth, resulting in the number 59,163

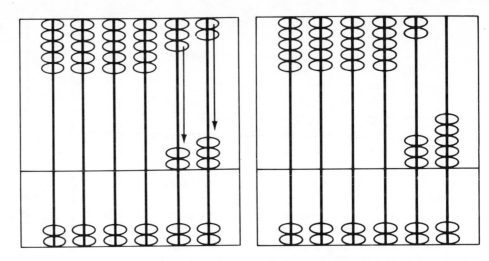

Figure X-8. How to add with an abacus: A simple problem for the beginning abacus user is to add 23 and 12. In the left-hand sketch, the abacus is set up to read "23". The arrows show that to add 12, we move a single bead in the 10s column and 2 beads in the ones column. The resulting abacus display (at right) gives the answer: 35

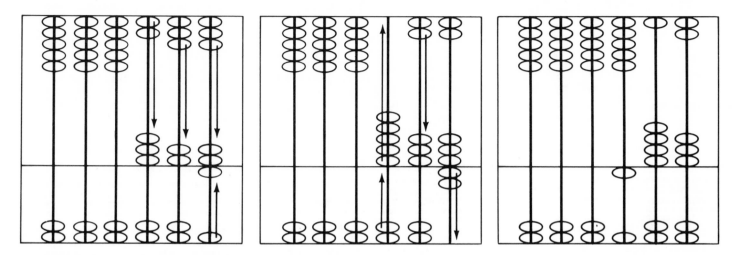

Figure X-9. Here's a slightly more complicated problem:
327 + 216 = ?

First set up 327, shown at far left. The arrows show how you
move various beads to add 2 to the 100s column, 1 to the 10s,
and 6 (one 5 plus 1) to the ones column.

In the center sketch, however, we see that the resulting number
is hard to read because the ones column reads "13". There
shouldn't ever be more than 9 in any one column. So as the
arrows show, we pull down the two "5" beads, so that the ones
column reads "3". Pulling down a single bead in the 10s column
replaces the 10 we just "subtracted" from the ones column.
In the 100s column, we have a total of 5 beads pulled to the
center, but this number (500) could just as well be expressed by a
single one of the bottom "5" beads, which would replace the top
5 "ones." In the right-hand sketch is displayed the answer: 543

you'll have to explain that it is simply a pictorial representation of any number from 0 up to 999,999, and that each column of beads represents another digit in the number. If they haven't learned fully that in our number system, the right-hand digit represents the number of *units* (or "ones") in a number, the second digit from the right represents the number of "tens," and so forth, there's a way of helping that along. You can write in "1," "10," "100," "1,000," and so on above each line of beads.

Hold the abacus so that the portion with five beads is on top. The top beads each represent one. Your digit is shown by the number of beads pushed toward the divider. If you move two beads toward the divider, you are showing "2" on the abacus. If you move five beads toward the center, you're showing "5." But there's another way to show "5."

Each bead on the bottom portion is worth five. So instead of pushing all five of the top beads, you can simply shove one of the bottom beads toward the center.

To add on the abacus, simply shove the proper number of beads *toward* the center. To subtract, you shove the proper number of beads *away from* the center. By the time I could finish explaining in English how to use an abacus, you could probably have it all figured out on your own. Give it a try. If all else fails, the nearby sketches will lend a hand. But be prepared to build more than one abacus, because once the kids get their hands on this one, they won't let you have it back!

BRAIN GAMES: SUPER CHECKERS AND CHESS

(Age 7 and up to play and build.)
Skills: Very easy.
Materials: Miscellaneous found art materials.

Checkers, at least as it's being played by a lot of kids these days, only vaguely resembles the game our Granddaddies played on a board held on their knees while they perched on nail kegs at the crossroads stores. Remember how, when we played the game, any checker that advanced to the opposite end of the board became a king? To make it a king, we piled an extra checker on top. Unlike regular checkers, which slide forward only, the king could slide or "jump" forward or backward.

Now, according to Great Neck's Super Checkers player Jeff Kesselman, youngsters are keeping up with the times by giving kings the chance to become super-kings (read "queens" if you wish). If a king is maneuvered all the way back to the last row on the side of the board it came from, and then *again* the full length of the board, back to the opposite side, it becomes a super-king, or—as novices call it—triple-king, since it stands three checkers high.

A super-king can move to any adjacent *red or black* square. It can "jump" and capture any adjacent piece of an opponent. It can jump over any adjacent piece of its own color. And a super-king can be captured only by another super-king.

One common complaint among Super Checkers players is that the triple-high checkers topple over. Being toy designers, we can quickly come up with a solution from

Figure X-10. Whether from plastic, hardware store pick-ups, wood, or found objects, youngsters of all ages can enjoy making their own personal chess sets

our boxes holding sundry bits of wood, hardware, and similar valuables. One simple way is to make checkers out of spindle spacers. Color one set, leave the other natural. Add maybe a dozen short lengths of dowels to the set of checkers. When a checker has advanced to king, a player shoves a dowel into the spacer's hole and can then stack one or two additional spacers on top without any danger of the king or super-king getting accidentally dethroned. No doubt your own hardware store and your own imagination can come up with some local variations.

Chess, a most ancient game, surpasses even Super Checkers when it comes to intellectual challenge. Youngsters from the age of maybe 7 on up aren't too young to match wits against a chess partner. But, how do you interest hyperactive young minds in sitting at a chess board for the time it takes to learn the intricate moves? Fair question!

One solution is to *build their own* fancy, personalized chess sets out of found objects. If Kate likes mechanics, for example, spend an hour with her in a hardware store until she assembles enough gadgets to make her own nuts-and-bolts chess set. It'll cost a dollar or two. Of if Robert goes wild over plastic, give him several bucks and an hour with you in a plastic retail shop. Together you'll find enough components to build a chess set of Robert's own design. Or if Jo's bananas over wood, several dollars and an hour later you and Jo should emerge from a lumber supplier with enough wood turnings and finials to assemble sixteen very personal chess pieces.

You don't have to assemble a set of white chess movers and a set of black chess movers for each child. There's no logical reason why the "black" chess movers have to be identical to the "white" movers. If one side uses wood and the other uses sculpted wire movers, that's really OK, as long as a queen is identifiable as a queen, a pawn as a pawn, and so on. There are only three provisos that I can think of. 1) You must design a chess set that contains all of the required chess pieces. 2) The children's "found" pieces must be easily recognizable to other players. 3) Your would-be chess designers will have to learn what they'll need before they shop for it. So they may have to play a couple of games on a borrowed set before setting off in search of found art objects to turn into chess pieces. It can also mean a trip to the library, where the shelves are full of generally fine books about how to play chess.

For fledglings or experienced chess players who need a review, here's a list of the required pieces for each side:
1 King (generally the largest piece).
1 Queen (generally a bit smaller than king).
2 Knights (which traditionally resemble horses or knights).
2 Bishops (which traditionally resemble bishops' hats).
2 Rooks (which traditionally resemble castles).
8 Pawns (which are the smallest pieces, as a rule).
Chess sets are so quickly assembled from found art that you may find yourself building several sets.

11 *Puppets and people*

I don't have to tell any parent or teacher how important a doll is to young children. They cuddle, carry, scold, teach, and talk to it. By the time kids reach about 4, they're ready for a doll that encourages a different kind of play. True, they may still want one or more of the cuddly variety—but puppets of various kinds offer dimensions to children's play that, these days, too many adults forget about. Let's correct that right now.

We're going to learn how to build different types of puppets and marionettes. *Marionettes* are manipulated via strings from above. *Puppets* can be manipulated from several angles and with hands, sticks, or other devices. You and the children, together or separately, can make from each type an infinite number of variations. You can create a puppet population explosion if you've a mind to.

Puppets and marionettes, because of the way they're constructed and regarded, invite drama in many children. Puppets are more likely to talk back than dolls. They're more apt to do things "on their own." With two puppets, a child can have a good friend and a misbehaving friend at the same time.

A child can talk to herself via a puppet, telling herself things she needs to have reinforced from some outside, objective third party. Depending on parent-child or teacher-child relationships, a puppet might be able to talk back to an adult when the child feels inhibited about talking back himself. Likewise, two or more children can talk candidly to each other via their puppets. If all the world's a stage and each of us players, then it's worthwhile—as well as a lot of fun—to have some puppets onstage with us.

All the puppets shown here will provide a lively medium for dramatic acting-out. Some are more limiting,

Figure XI-1. With two ordinary rubber balls and a wooden dowel, you can make a very simple Stickball Puppet

such as the Pinocchio version of the balloon-and-papier-mâché-puppet. Some encourage greater physical dexterity, such as the marionettes. A few—the stickball puppet, for example—can be finished in minutes, which is important for younger, impatient minds. Some have to be started one day to be played with the next, which is good training in patience. But none of them is difficult or expensive. Four-year-olds can play with them, six-year-olds can make them with adult assistance, and ten-year-olds can build many of them unassisted.

STICKBALL PUPPET

(3 to 8 to play with; 8 and up to build.)
Skills: Extremely easy; ideal first project.
Materials: ½″ wooden dowels; "pinkie" rubber balls; old socks.

One of the fastest puppets you'll ever build, this one requires only two rubber handballs (the "pinkie" is ideal), an old sock, a stick (such as a 1′ length of ½″ thick or ⅜″ thick wooden dowel) plus some household odds and ends. Two golf tees make dandy arms.

Cut a hole in one rubber ball just a bit smaller than the thickness of your dowel stick. Put a liberal blob of glue at the end of the stick and quickly shove it straight into the ball until the gluey end rests on the inside, opposite the hole. Prop it up carefully until the glue dries. With a fast-setting product, it should be dry by the time you've finished the next step.

In the other rubber ball, cut two holes for the dowel in

both opposite ends. Think of the process as making openings for the north-south pole to stick through the rubber "earth." Then cut off an old sock above the heel— the more colorful the sock, the better. Discard the "foot" part and slip the sock "dress" over the rubber-ball body, securing it at the neck with a few drops of glue. Photos demonstrate the process.

Shove the body onto the dowel stick and use a few drops of glue to fasten the dressed body to the bare head. Poke two golf tees partway into the upper part of the body as arms. Glue will *help* hold the tees in place— but if you're worried about kids pulling them loose, then it's best you make your puppets *without* arms. Or alternatively, you can buy some telephone cable or #12 insulated electrical wire (described in Chapter 7, where we discussed clothes-pin people). Shove a 6″ length of the wire through matching holes on each side of the body and twist the two ends into hands.

You'll want a face on the puppet, no doubt. The easiest way is to use ball-point pens—red for the lips, black for the eyes, nose, and eyebrows. Nail polish, paint, or magic markers help you make nice faces, too. If you want a funny face, shove in a golf tee for a nose. With the pens or paints, you can sketch hair onto the rubber ball head, or you can create fuzzy hair by glueing yarn or string on top.

The kids will probably know how to use stick puppets in dramatic play. For adults, here's the secret. You crouch behind a table, desk, living-room chair, or similar "stage." Then, out of sight, you can hold on to the sticks while your puppets dance, run, jump, and talk.

PUPPET ON A STICK

(3 to 8 to play with; 4 and up to build.)
Skills: Extremely easy; ideal first project.
Materials: Wooden dowel; finial; maybe some spindle spacers.

Here's a stick puppet you can make in less time even than the stickball model. All you need is a dowel stick and a wooden finial such as lumberyards and hardware stores sell for making spindle furniture. You might want to add a few spacers for the body and some small dowels or heavy wire for arms.

Finials come in several different shapes, all of them suitable for heads. Glue one to the top of a dowel stick 12″ or 16″ long, and wide enough to fit snugly into the finial's hole. If you want to, slip several spacers onto the dowel just beneath the head and glue them there. Golf tees glued into small holes in the top spacer make dandy arms; they even have "hands" preattached. Small dowel sticks used with beads make safe arms for older children. For flexible arms, use electric wire (technique shown in Chapter 7).

I like to leave the puppets on sticks unpainted, adding colored yarn for hair, and using ball-point pens or paint to sketch on simple eyes and mouth. But that's about all. However, if paint you must, go to it!

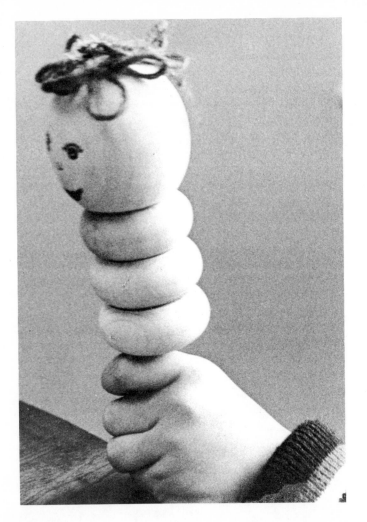

SOCK-IT-TO-'EM HAND PUPPET

(3 to 8 to play with; 8 and up to build.)
Skills: Easy.
Materials: Old socks, sundry yarn or thread.

Shove a sock all the way onto your left hand. Be sure the heel is on your knuckles. Separate your left thumb from the rest of your fingers. Using your right index finger, push the sock into the hollow between your left thumb and fingers; that's the puppet's mouth! Gather up the loose folds around your "mouth" and stitch them firmly into place, being careful not to attach a finger permanently to the puppet. (If you're left-handed, stitch the sock-puppet on your right hand.)

Sew a couple of buttons securely in place for the eyes. And then, using yarn or embroidery floss, stitch some hair onto the head and even sew on some whiskers, too. Nothing says all puppets have to be cute. If you're worried that the mouth doesn't look mouth-like enough, sew some bright red fabric in the appropriate place at the same time you form the mouth with your needle and thread. But kids I've seen *know* where the mouth is, no matter what the color.

Figure XI-2. There's nothing lacking in Oscar's super-simple Puppet-on-a-Stick

BIG BUT HOLLOW-HEADED PUPPETS

(6 and up to play with; 8 and up to build.)
Skills: Easy enough, but patience is a virtue here.
Materials: Glue, balloon, old newspaper, old sock.

These are kind of messy, which is fun in itself if you're in there working with your kids. You're going to use liquid glue and old newspapers to form a hollow papier-mâché puppet head large enough that a child's (or adult's) hand will fit inside. Papier-mâché is cheap, lightweight, easily colored, and amazingly tough—especially since we use modern glue instead of old-fashioned flour and water paste. But how to form the gooey stuff into a head?

The trick is to start with a balloon. Blow it up as big as you want the head to be—around 6″ in diameter is good for your first one. Then grab some old newspapers and tear them up into strips 1″ wide. Next mix up a mixture of about two parts of Elmer's Glue-All (or similar product) to one part of water. The mixture should be about as thick as heavy cream.

Soak one strip of newspaper in the paste and then wrap it around the balloon. Since the glue doesn't hold well onto the balloon, the ends of the strip have to overlap. Repeat the soak-and-wrap process, laying down each new strip at a different angle so eventually you have the entire balloon wrapped in gluey paper.

Don't stop with just one layer. Keep soaking and wrapping until you've covered the balloon with three or four layers of paper. Then set the head aside to dry thoroughly. Warning: don't put it in a spot that's much warmer than the room where you started working, or the balloon will try to expand, and that can give your puppet a *splitting* headache.

After the head has dried, use a knife or razor blade to cut a hole in the bottom of it. The hole should be about 3″, or just wide enough for a hand to slip through. (The balloon's going to pop, and you can pull it out of your puppet head now.)

Find an old sock and slice the area just from the toe to the heel into strips about 1″ wide. Cut from the toe toward the heel. (Don't slice *off* the strips!) Using a product like Elmer's Glue-All, glue the strips of sock to the inside of your puppet head. When it's dry, the ankle and leg part of the sock will hide the child's hand and also serve as a body.

Paint eyes, nose, and mouth onto the puppet. Glue on some yarn for hair, or add a small hat. With scrap cloth, you can make a dress or cape, too, if you like.

As you and the children get better at making papier-mâché puppets, you can add limitless sophistication. You can form a nose and ears out of paper and glue at the same time you make the basic head. You can make papier-mâché hair or a hat an integral part of the head.

Here's a wrinkle that's lots of fun: Poke a hole where the nose should be. Then an appropriately placed finger can become the nose, wiggling during dialogue or growing longer, and longer, and longer during lies.

You can poke holes in the body-sock, too. Then a thumb and an index finger, or a thumb and little finger, can become hands for the hollow-headed puppet.

Another way to make your puppet is first to set the blown-up balloon into the open top of a small, empty oatmeal box. Wrap the first strips of papier-mâché from

the box, over the top of the balloon, and back down to the box. The gluey strips will stick to the paper box, so you won't have to worry about overlapping them. Be sure to lay down several layers of papier-mâché over the balloon, but only one or two layers will suffice for the box. Don't cut the bottom off the oatmeal box until after the glue has dried. Then the box will become the puppet's body.

SIMPLE ALL-WOOD MARIONETTE

(3 and up to use; 7 and up to build.)
Skills: Very simple; a good first project.
Materials: Tiny scraps of lumber; spindle spacers; wooden dowels; string.

In terms of construction, this is just a collection of simple wooden parts tied together into a marionette. But in visual terms this marionette and its variations provide an exciting exercise in learning *how we see*. All of the parts we build with are identical whether we want a dog, a duck, or a damsel.

If you're standing on a country road and see something coming way down the road, you can't see if it has skin, fur, or feathers, and probably you can't see the features on its face. Maybe you can't even tell if it has two legs or four. Still, most of the time you can identify the type

Figure XI-3. Jason's papier-mâché puppet won't have to do without a nose for very long...
*   ...because he simply pushes a finger through the appropriate hole and presto! Like Pinocchio's, the "nose" grows*

of creature it is, based on angle of the back plus location of the feet and head. These are exactly the dissimilarities used in constructing this set of marionettes.

Heads and feet are made from circles of wood. If you're lazy like me, use spacers from the spindle-furniture section of your lumber or hardware store. Otherwise you can cut slices from a wooden closet pole or saw circles from pieces of pine or hardwood.

All of the bodies are semicircles of wood. And to make our visual point, all of these marionettes should have the same size bodies. If you're working with heads and feet made from spacers or closet poles, which are about 1¾" in diameter, semicircles cut from 4" lumber (resulting in a diameter of about 3½") are about ideal.

After all of the parts are cut out and sanded, you can assemble the marionettes. I prefer to use ⅛" nylon rope, which not only holds the feet and hands on to the bodies but doubles as reasonably thick arms and legs. Whenever possible, I like to tie my rope through the spacers' holes and drill holes into the wooden semicircles for the rope to thread through. If that doesn't catch your fancy, however, you can staple the rope into place or screw ¾" screw eyes into the appropriate places and run the rope through them. Then simple knots will secure the ropes to the spacers and semicircles.

Figure XI-4. This dog marionette is made from some of the simplest hardware-store objects. With the same materials, you can make a person (by making the back erect) or a duck (by slanting the back). You don't have to use such heavy strings as these, but why try to hide the fact that it's a marionette?

Figure XI-5. Two dowels, crossed and lashed, are the simplest means of marionette manipulation

The angle of the body piece is very important to the visual impact of these marionettes. The dog's body has to be very nearly horizontal, the human's body very nearly vertical (unless you want an old person, in which case the cliché calls for a slightly tilted body). The duck's body should slope about 45 degrees. So in most cases, don't trust just one string to the controls to support the body—fasten one string to each end of the semicircle whenever possible. Nearby pictures show how.

I like to keep the controls simple for younger children, just lashing together into a cross two pieces of 10″ long dowel sticks. I see no reason to use delicate black threads on the controls in an effort to disguise the fact that these are marionettes. I prefer rather heavy cord that doesn't get tangled or broken easily. As children get older and their dexterity improves along with their flair for puppetry, you can separate the two control sticks so the legs can be controlled with one hand, the rest of the marionette with the other.

I'd like to see these marionettes left in their natural-wood state. Most kids quickly enough decide that one is a dog or cat—maybe varying the animal from day to day. Children versed in mythology may decide it's a unicorn! Young, uncluttered minds often know immediately that another is a duck or a chicken. And the person looks right even to most adults.

12 Rocking, rolling, and climbing toys

These days it seems as if everybody's gotta have a ride-'em toy. Mom and Pop run out to the car dealer every couple of years to buy a new set of wheels, discarding the still usable older model. Junior gets his own kiddy car early in life, and when he's older, a rocking horse. Bicycle and soapbox racer replace the rocking horse until Junior is old enough to have a car. That's the usual progression.

But if you're trying to instill some sense of ecological and economic sense in your kids, you can buy a set of wheels plus a few boards and build your own horse that rolls in the early years, then rocks and grows taller as little legs grow. Later on, you and Junior can use the wheels to build a rugged soapbox racer.

A BASIC HORSE

(12 and up to build.)
Skills: A little demanding; not an ideal first project.
Materials: 1" x 8" pine or hardwood, 7' long.
1" x 4" pine or hardwood, 19" long.
Glue.
2" casing nails or 1¾" flathead wood screws.

Riding and rocking toys are perfectly safe if they're well designed. Throughout this book, I've encouraged you to vary my dimensions and shapes at will, but here I encourage you to follow the dimensions and layout carefully. This one is designed so the wheels or the rocking legs extend substantially outside the center of gravity in every direction. That means that if you follow my directions closely, it'll be tough to tip over one of these horses.

127

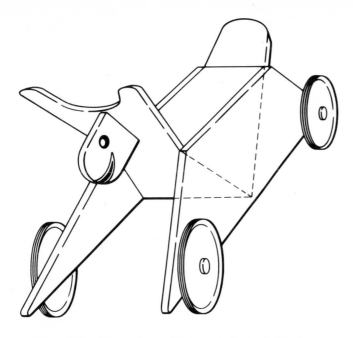

Figure XII-1. A basic horse. You can make it a hobby horse as shown here, ideal for older children. Or, using the same body, it can be a rocking horse or rocking pony—smaller and even safer for very young wranglers. (The dotted lines show how the horse's "head" and "tail" extend right down to the animal's stomach, making the construction very stable and secure)

The top or "seat" of this horse is a 15" long piece of 1" x 4" board. I like the feel and looks of hardwood, but it's tough to find, expensive to buy, and harder to work than pine. Pine won't let you down, so if you have any doubts, that's the material to use.

The sides are cut from 1" x 8" boards. The top of each side is 15" long, of course. Each end tapers at 45 degrees, resulting in a bottom edge of 30".

Head and tail pieces are also the horse's internal supports. Since the top of the horse is not as thick as the bottom, the head and tail supports have to be tapered. You'll see how to cut the simple shapes in the nearby Figure XII-2.

If you look closely at how the body of this horse tapers outward from top to bottom, you'll see how you must sand or use a SurForm tool or plane to taper the edges of the 4" board for the top. About 3/16" of the bottom edge of that piece has to be cut away so everything will fit together snugly.

Assemble the horse using both glue and nails or screws. First fasten the sides loosely to the head-and-tail frame. Put the top piece into position to make sure that the head, tail, top, and both sides fit together properly. At this point, you can still force the frame a bit further apart or together if need be. When everything fits, fasten the top to the sides, the head to the top, the tail to the top, and finally the sides to the frame. Glue and nail the nose into place last.

By the time you've fastened your horse together, you should already have done the major amount of sanding. You're bound to make some knicks and scrapes and smear

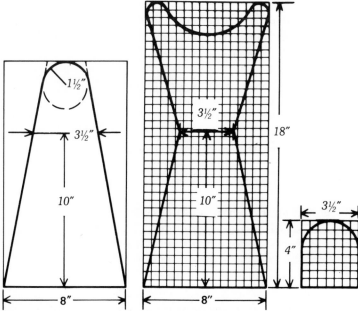

1½"

3½"

10"

8"

3½"

18"

3½"

10"

8"

3½"

4"

Figure XII-3. Your horse's body (below) assembles like this. The two body pieces are each 30" long on the bottom, 15" long on top. Cut these from a board 8" wide

Figure XII-2. At left, the tail assembly for your basic horse body. Cut it from an 8" wide piece of lumber, 14" long. The 3½" width indicated matches the approximate width of a "four-inch" board which is generally very close to 3½" wide
The head of your horse (center) is cut from an 18" length of 8" wide lumber
The nose (right) doesn't have to be any special size, but the dimensions shown here will work nicely. Don't leave the nose off, however, since it serves as a brace, strengthening the head piece which is likely to get a lot of twisting from young cowpokes

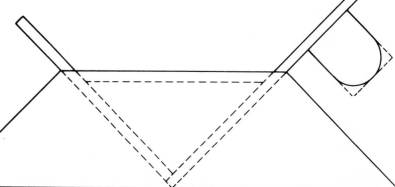

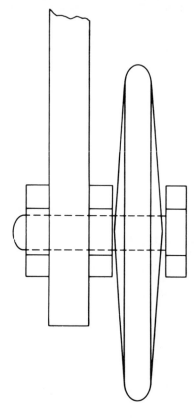

Figure XII-4. How to fasten wheels to the body pieces of the horse

some glue while building the horse, so do touch-up sanding before you tackle the finishing. And don't drill holes for your wheels until you buy them; axle holes vary so much in size that you can't plan ahead.

You can finish off this horse with clear urethane to give it a natural-wood finish, or paint it with child-proof enamels. White is a common color, but there's nothing wrong with a horse of a different color. If you want to paint on eyes and a mouth, don't forget that a horse's mouth, unlike ours, is part of its long nose.

HOBBYHORSE

(1 to 3 years to play with; 12 and up to build.)
Skills: Not terribly demanding.
Materials: Set of wheels plus "Basic Horse."

After building the basic horse, you have to put it on rockers or wheels. First we'll tackle the wheels, thus making a hobbyhorse or kiddy car whose seat is 8 or 9″ off the floor.

I prefer 8″ wheels of solid metal with rubber tires—which are a bit tough to find in many local hardware stores. But it's quite easy to find 6″ wheels, and 4″ wheels are a snap. For a kiddy car, the 4″ variety is OK; but if you plan to use the wheels later for a soapbox racer, the larger wheels are definitely your better choice.

Assuming your wheels have a ½″ hole through their center, invest in four ½″ *machine bolts*. The bolts should be just long enough to reach through the wheel, through the board, and through *two nuts*. (Buy your bolts at the same time you buy your wheels so you don't have to guess about correct fit.)

Figure XII-4 shows how to mount each wheel using one bolt and two nuts. If you select the bolts carefully, they will be just long enough to fit inside the last nut but not protrude more than ¼". The nuts, resting alongside the wood as they do, are quite harmless. But an extended length of bolt could conceivably cause minor injury. Tighten each nut so that it grabs firmly onto the wood but not overly tightly onto the wheel. If the wheels spin easily when mounted, the horse is ready to ride.

ROCKING PONY

(2 to 4 to play with; 12 and up to build.)
Skills: Not tough, but careful attention to detail is required.
Materials: 8' of 1" x 6" pine or hardwood.
10' of 1" x 4" pine or hardwood.

Take off the wheels (but save them), set the horse onto a rocking platform, and your rocking horse is ready, Sire. Or, since we're going to start with a little horse for wobbly-legged toddlers, let's call it a Rocking Pony.

The two rockers are cut from the 1" x 6" lumber. Cut the 8' long piece in half. Then clamp or temporarily nail both halves together so you can easily saw out two identically curved rockers. Using a grid of 1" squares, sketch the curve in Figure XII-7 onto your top piece of lumber. Then saw both at once. A sabre saw is the easiest tool to use, but a coping or keyhole saw, if worked patiently, will do fine.

From the 1 x 4s, cut four pieces 18" long and one piece that's 16½" long. Consult Figure XII-5 and install the cross braces accurately into place so that they will support the rocking horse's legs now in their low position and later when they're higher up. Use glue and either nails or screws to hold the crosspieces onto the rockers.

Figure XII-6 shows how to cut the short legs needed to hold the Rocking Pony on to the platform. Slip the slotted end onto the appropriate crosspiece, shove the flat end up against the tail brace or head brace, line up the hole in the leg with the hole in the body (where a wheel would go), and slip a 2" long bolt through the hole. Tighten the nut and move on to the next leg.

After the four legs have been bolted in place, I'd put a screw through the slotted end of each leg, extending into the crosspiece. The slots themselves handle all of the stresses and strains; the screws simply keep your young wrangler from lifting the horse off the platform. (If you don't cover the screw hole with plastic wood, you can easily convert this Rocking Pony into a Rocking Horse later on.)

I haven't forgotten to tell you to nail or screw the flat end of each leg to the tail brace and head brace. From a design standpoint, it isn't necessary. The flat end of leg resting against the flat brace can't move as long as the bolt and the slotted end are in place. Nevertheless, I'm sure many parents and teachers will add at least one nail or screw to each leg-end.

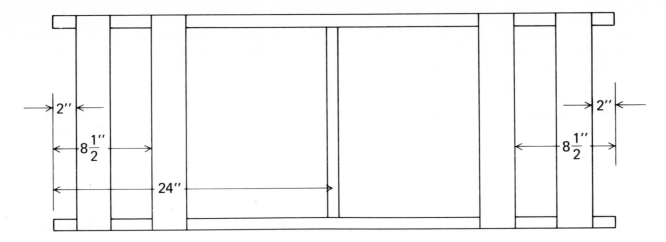

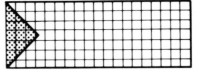

Figure XII-5. To turn the horse into a rocker, here are the dimensions of the platform you want to build. Use 2" x 6" lumber for the rockers, 1" x 4" lumber for the braces. Simply sketch a smoothly curving line onto one of the 48" long boards, and clamp or nail a second board to it so that you can cut two rockers at once. (That 48" length was chosen to keep the horse from tipping. Likewise, the extra-wide platform keeps even chubby children from leaning over far enough to topple their mount sideways)

Figure XII-6. For youngsters just being introduced to rocking horses, start with the shorter 10½" legs shown at top. For older youngsters, make longer 17½" legs, according to the pattern at bottom. Either way, you'll need 4 legs in all

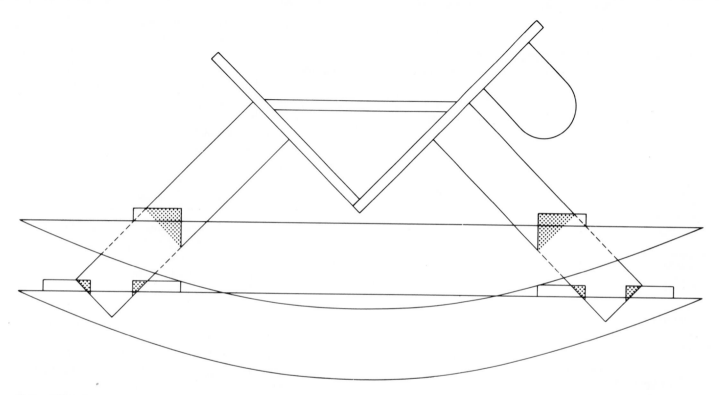

Figure XII-7. Assemble the rocking pony (short legs) or rocking horse (long legs) by aligning the legs to the platform as shown

ROCKING HORSE

(4 to 10 to play with; 12 and up to build.)
Skills: Not tough, but careful attention to detail is required.
Materials: Four pieces, 17½", 1" x 4" pine or hardwood in addition to earlier construction projects in this chapter.

To convert the smaller Rocking Pony to this bigger horse, all you need do is cut out four pieces of the longer legs shown in Figure XII-6. Assemble the legs onto the platform according to Figures XII-7 and the rocking horse is ready to ride.

SOAPBOX RACER

(10 and up to play with; 12 and up to build—10 and up with adult guidance.)
Skills: Easier than it looks, but careful measurements are helpful.
Materials: 1" x 12" pine board, 10' long.
1" x 4" pine board, 12' long.
½" x 6" machine bolts, four pieces.
½" nuts, ten pieces.
½" x 3" machine bolt.
Dozen ½" washers.
1½" screw eyes, four pieces.
6' of ¼" nylon rope.

The body of this racer is a 4' long piece of 12" wide pine board. The seat back is cut from an 18" long piece of the 12" pine. The upper 6" are rounded off into a semicircle. (Draw a half circle by using a 6" radius.)

Two armrests for the seat are 12" square pieces, rounded off. Use a 12" radius circle to draw the curve.

The streamlined front of the racer is made from three pieces of the 12" pine, each 8" long. Use the same 12" radius circle to draw the curves: just put the point of the compass or string about 4" off the piece of wood so the curve moves smoothly from corner to corner. Use glue and nails to hold all of the parts together.

Next you can start to assemble the axles. A single board would not be rigid enough to support a large child and would flex from the weight, rub against the underside of the racer's body, and make steering difficult. So reinforce the single 4" board with a second 4" board fastened together at right angles. In order to fasten the wheels to each end, you need two more pieces of 1" x 4" lumber for each end of the axle. One is glued and nailed at the end of the "L" and the other about 3" from the end. Figure XII-9 shows how the end of the axle and wheels look as you assemble them.

Assuming the wheels you bought have approximately ½" holes, drill matching ½" holes through the axle braces. Shove a bolt through each wheel and secure it with a ½" nut. Shove the bolt into the first axle hole and install another nut. As you tighten the nut, the bolt will gradually extend through the hole in the second axle brace. The two nuts should grab tightly against the wood, leaving the wheel free to spin on the bolt. Another nut secures the bolt to the inside axle brace.

The front axle is 36" long, the rear axle 18" long. Glue

Figure XII-8. You and your kids can make this modern version of a soapbox racer in a single weekend of fun. You don't even need a genuine soapbox!

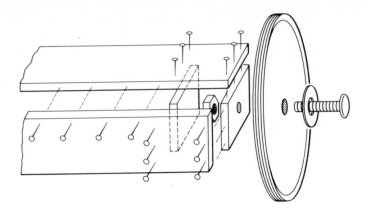

Figure XII-9. If your racer is to withstand the rigors of hard riding, the axle and wheel assembly is quite important. This is the ideal way to assemble yours

and nail the rear axle to the bottom of the racer. The front axle has to pivot as a means of steering. Drill a ½" hole through the exact center of your axle. Drill a matching ½" hole about 4" from the front of the racer's body. Slip the 3" long machine bolt through the racer body, install a nut, and then slip the bolt through the axle, adding another nut. After you allow enough slack for the bolt to turn easily in the hole through the racer body, tighten the two nuts so they grab the axle tightly.

Washers help moving parts slip easily over each other. When you assemble your racer, you should slip washers between the wheels and bolts, between the nut holding onto the top of the axle and the bottom of your racer's body, and in similar locations. A dab of grease or petroleum jelly will provide adequate, clean lubrication.

Strong rope, such as ¼" nylon, helps to make a good steering mechanism. Screw in a 1½" screw eye near each end of your front axle. Install matching screw eyes near the front of the racer's body, outside the area covered by the "hood." After threading your rope through the body screw eyes, tie the ends securely to the two axle screw eyes. When that's done, all that's left is to paint the racer, install your official number, and take a test spin down a gentle hill far away from traffic.

CLIMBER SWING

(3 to 10 to play with; adults should build.)
Skills: *Easy if you have the patience to drill over a dozen holes, tie over a dozen knots, and measure accurately.*
Materials: *Nine pieces of 1" wooden dowel, each 12" long. 25' of ¼" nylon rope. Two pieces of 2½" screw eyes.*

Kids love to climb. Kids love to swing. Kids love ropes. But parents wonder if they're safe.

I can guarantee you a perfectly safe rope ladder that doubles as a swing, and at a budget price. (In case you have any doubts; this entire rope ladder is constructed from one piece of rope. That way you don't have to worry about any of your knots coming unfastened.) You can hang it from a ceiling, doorway, or tree, and move it about if you want. I designed and built mine when David was only 3. He couldn't climb very far back then, *and he knew it.* Like most kids, he quickly and safely found his limits and stayed within them, while always testing a bit to see if he was ready to climb one step higher or swing a few inches further out. By age 6, he could pull himself all the way to the top and swing as far as he wanted to on any rung. He's never fallen. After we watched him playing the first few days, we were never afraid of his hurting himself.

When you buy a rope ladder like this through some educational toy stores or catalogues, it's unbelievably expensive. But the only materials needed to make it are wooden dowels and nylon rope.

After cutting your hardwood dowels into 12" lengths, drill parallel ¼" holes about ½" from each end. Using sandpaper or a SurForm tool, smooth off the ends of the dowels; they don't have to be rounded completely unless you prefer them that way.

The materials and sketch here are for a rope ladder about 8' high. That's about ideal for mounting to the ceiling in newer houses. If you have higher ceilings, you may have to expand the dimensions for rope and add to the number of dowels. (Do the opposite to mount this project to something like a 7' doorway.)

Whatever you do, please don't simply stretch the space between the rungs to make the ladder longer or shorter. Don't shorten the length of the rungs. Don't skip a rung or two near the top, simply running a couple feet of rope up to the ceiling or wherever else you mount this device. The dimensions have been carefully designed to prevent a child, either accidentally or on purpose, from making loops in the ladder and shoving his head into them. I was horrified to find this safety feature lacking in some of the store-bought versions!

To assemble the parts, stretch the rope out on the floor and get all of the kinks out of it. Fold it exactly in half. Thread one end of the rope into one hole in your bottom dowel, and thread the other end into the other hole. Slide the bottom dowel all the way down the rope until it pulls the rope taut between its two holes.

On each of the two free portions of the rope, measure 12" from the bottom dowel and tie a knot. Since you should be slipping ¼" rope through a ¼" hole, a simple single knot should be sufficient. If your holes are substantially oversized, however, you may have to double up your knots to keep them from slipping through the holes.

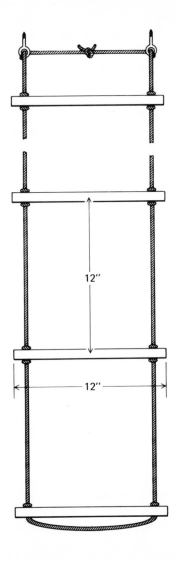

Thread your next dowel onto the rope and pull it down to the knots. Measure, knot, and thread all of the following dowels until the rope ladder is fully assembled.

The screw eyes that hold up this ladder have to be secured in *solid* wood. That means if you plan to hang it from a ceiling, you have to locate one of the wooden 2 x 4s under the plaster. Most doorways, especially the ones that have wooden trim around them, have a solid wooden understructure.

Screw eyes of the size we're using are hard to install unless you drill a pilot hole. Generally a ¼″ hole is ideal, but check the screw eyes you've purchased to see if that size is large enough to allow you to turn the hardware in as far as it can go, but not so large as to undermine the threads that the screw eye should cut into the wood as it goes in.

Fasten the screw eyes 11″ apart. Slip the loose ends of rope through the screw eyes and pull up the slack until the bottom rung is about 8″ off the floor. Wrap the rope around each "eye" three times, then pull the two loose ends together and tie them in a simple square knot. That's probably the most secure way there is to fasten the top of this rope ladder. Tension on the rope can make the square knot only tighter, never looser. If you try to tie some exotic or complicated knot, unless you really know knots well, you can't be certain that it will hold indefinitely. To keep little hands from fooling with the knot, I like to fasten the loose ends to the top rope with strapping tape.

Figure XII-10. A combination rope ladder and swing that's safe, rugged, and fun. To insure maximum safety, use the materials specified in the text and assemble them carefully, following the dimensions shown here

Some adult should take a test swing on this swinging rope ladder. Stand on the bottom rung and bounce up and down a few times. The rope will stretch somewhat—it's supposed to. The bottom rung should not reach the floor, however. If it does, you'll have to tie the ladder higher off the ground.

When the test romp is completed, turn it over to the kids. You'll want to keep a close eye on it for the first few days. And every so often afterwards, check that the rope is still tied properly, that the knots below the dowels are not forcing up through the holes, and that nothing is wearing out. But I wish all toys took as little attention as this one. After many years of use, sometimes getting hours of hard treatment in a single day at the hands of half a dozen different kids, the original model of this swinging rope ladder has yet to need repair or even readjustment.

Index